T0067172

BEEN THERE, DONE THAT, WROTE THIS!

A Personal Journey Through
Chronic Illness, Bullies, and
Spirituality

MICHELEANNE

BALBOA.
PRESS

A DIVISION OF HAY HOUSE

Balboa Press books may be ordered through booksellers or by contacting:

Balboa Press
A Division of Hay House
1663 Liberty Drive
Bloomington, IN 47403
www.balboapress.com
1 (877) 407-4847

Because of the dynamic nature of the Internet, any web addresses or links contained in this book may have changed since publication and may no longer be valid. The views expressed in this work are solely those of the author and do not necessarily reflect the views of the publisher, and the publisher hereby disclaims any responsibility for them.

The author of this book does not dispense medical advice or prescribe the use of any technique as a form of treatment for physical, emotional, or medical problems without the advice of a physician, either directly or indirectly. The intent of the author is only to offer information of a general nature to help you in your quest for emotional and spiritual well-being. In the event you use any of the information in this book for yourself, which is your constitutional right, the author and the publisher assume no responsibility for your actions.

Any people depicted in stock imagery provided by Thinkstock are models, and such images are being used for illustrative purposes only.
Certain stock imagery © Thinkstock.

Print information available on the last page.

ISBN: 978-1-5043-8921-1 (sc)
ISBN: 978-1-5043-8922-8 (e)

Balboa Press rev. date: 10/12/2017

Prologue

I was initially inspired to write this book in order to help people who have been newly diagnosed with an illness deal with the initial shock. My goal was to show people how to be prepared to deal with life after diagnosis, and consequently, the many new challenges that will arise in life. Looking back I realize that this book has been inside me for years.

I see so many people on a regular basis who are hurting for so many different reasons. Chronic pain and illness cause suffering, and so do many other of life's experiences in general. Having overcome many difficulties of my own, from chronic illness, to dealing with bullies, to judgement and religious condemnation; I feel compelled to share some of my experiences. I sincerely hope that you gain some insight on how to overcome your own difficulties, and live your best life, with grace.

Contents

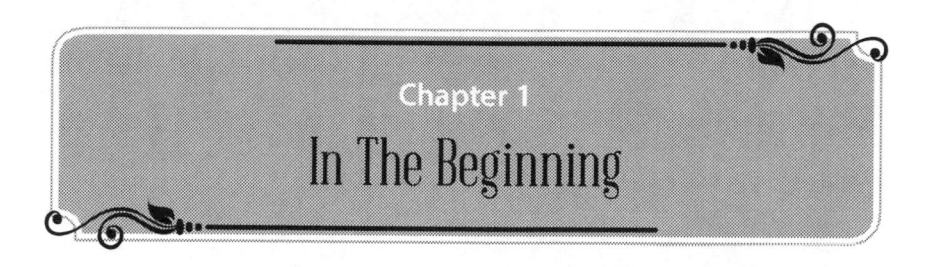

Chapter 1
In The Beginning

I arrived on November 8, 1975 around 5 pm. My lungs had merely developed to that of a 6-month-old fetus; the umbilical cord wrapped around my neck and tied in a knot. My parents tell me that I was turning blue and I was not expected to survive. In an effort to save my life, I spent the following 9 days in an incubator. I can only imagine how difficult it must have been for my parents to have to deal with the uncertainty of the survival of their firstborn child. It truly breaks my heart to think of what they must have gone through. Good news, I managed to survive, and I have always believed that there must be a reason. My life has certainly had its fair share of ups and downs, and I believe I have learned many lessons that I would like to share with you. As I have stated, my first 9 days I was to spend alone in an incubator, fighting to survive. Mom says I grew up on antibiotics, and Dad was always shoving a pill down my throat for something. I lived with severe allergies, eczema, and chronic infections. It was the beginning of my journey.

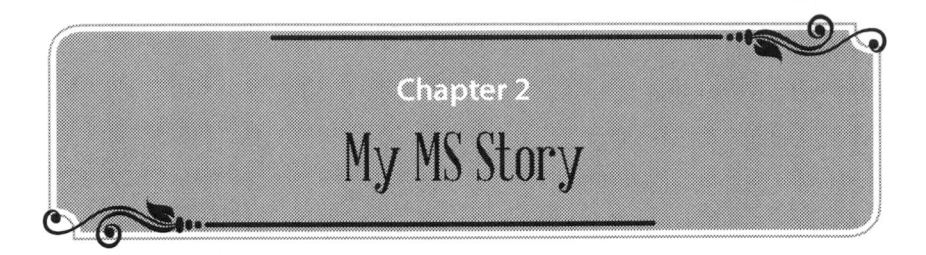

Chapter 2
My MS Story

During the spring of 1988, I had gone to see an ophthalmologist in Saint John. He was our family's eye doctor, and he prescribed new eye glasses for me. My family took me to the optician to pick up my new glasses. They brought my glasses out, all shiny and new, placed them on me and started making adjustments to have them fit perfectly. "How's that?" they asked.

Expecting to be able to see better, I was concerned that there were fields missing in my view, as though I had been staring at the sun. I kept blinking, straining to focus on something.

I replied, "I can't see."

My mom thought I was just being difficult. I certainly didn't blame her, I was a teenager, after all. But, I could not find the right words to explain how my vision was affected. It was as though I had been staring at a light bulb. So, I finally convinced my parents that I was not lying, and they called the ophthalmologist's office. I got in to see him immediately. I remember the part of the exam where I was asked to find the number or letter on a page of coloured dots. You should be able to see a number or a letter amongst the dots. My right eye was perfect; however, I could see nothing with my left eye. I remember the doctor

2

speaking closely with my parents about what could be causing what I heard him refer to as "Optic Neuritis".

In the following days, I was sent to see a specialist at a medical research center. I was given an MRI, followed by a neurological examination by a neurologist. The neurological exam revealed numbness in my hands, feet, and skin on my legs. I also had L'Hermitte's Phenomena, which is kind of like a shock wave sensation that happened every time I looked downward with my chin to chest.

I was not told anything other than they saw a "UBO - Unidentified Bright Object" at the base of my skull. I was prescribed Prednisone 12 tablets/day for five days, then 11/day, 10/day, etc., until gone, and then we will see. I don't recall getting a recheck.

While recovering from an unknown MS attack, and on Prednisone, my parents decided that we should take a vacation and go camping in the state of Maine, USA. We went with a family that was close friends with mine. While we were there, my parents decided to take me to a "church camp" to have me prayed over, for healing. I was not impressed. Why did I need prayer? My vision was getting better and so was everything else. I remember my father pointing at a set of crutches that were hanging high up on the wall. He told me that someone was healed of Multiple Sclerosis and did not need crutches anymore. "Wonderful, what does that have to do with me?" was my thought. I was then taken to the front of the church where people proceeded to pray for me.

Now remember, I was only 13 years old; I had no clue as to what Multiple Sclerosis even was, nor did I understand the crowd of complete strangers surrounding me, shouting and speaking in tongues while touching me. I had no idea what was going on. I was so angry... and it was not just because of the steroid rage from Prednisone. I felt vulnerable and violated. Needless to say, anytime I had numbness and tingling in my hands and feet, or any strange issues resembling what I had first experienced, I NEVER SAID A WORD.

Chapter 3

Hindsight Is 20/20

Over the years that followed, I can see now that I have experienced several MS symptoms, having done my research. I have had many head injuries due to poor balance. I had broken bones, sprains, and strains. I became the comic relief to everyone for being so clumsy. I even had a broken leg for my first day of school. I never really had colds or flu or "normal" illness, just all these weird, abnormal things that did not seem to happen to anyone else. I remember every time I would exercise, I thought that I could feel "fat cells bursting", which is what I told myself at the time to explain the tingling that I would feel in my legs, thighs and glutes. I had mistaken it as a good thing. I had never heard of what I now know as "the MS hug", which is a sensation like fluttering of muscles around your torso and butt. It feels almost like ginger ale being poured through your muscles, if you can imagine that. I can recall several times that I would wake up in excruciating pain in my lower back and stomach. My father would take me to the hospital's outpatient department, only to be sent away as they could never find the cause for the pain.

I remember at age seventeen, I went to the doctor because I could not void my bladder. My bladder was so full; my lower back and abdomen ached horribly. I felt as though I was going to blow up and almost wished

I would if it would relieve the agony that I was experiencing. My family doctor told me to take Robaxacet. Seriously. I explained, "I did not strain a muscle, I can't pee!" Again, he insisted Robaxacet would help. It did not. I had to teach myself how to physically manipulate my bladder until I could get something started. After countless bladder infections, I knew something was going on.

Hind-sight is truly amazing. I can probably count the number of times I had the flu. I rarely caught the "bug that was going around", but I lived with extreme allergies, and chronic infections unrelated to anything contagious. It was such a strange phenomenon, I was always somewhat ill, and was never really able to explain what the problem was. As I stated earlier, I was known as "the klutz" as I was always tripping, knocking things over, or dropping stuff. I have even lost count of the number of concussions I have had, as balance has never been my forte, so to speak. I joined the gym and greatly improved my strength; I practiced yoga and was extremely flexible, but it seemed that all my physical practice was in vain, as I would quickly seize up again. I suffered migraines from neck and shoulder spasms. I was always so tired. Not just tired, but I literally felt as though my limbs weighed a few hundred pounds each. When people tried to hold a conversation with me, it was all I could do to concentrate on what they were telling me, hoping there would not be a quiz afterwards. I had read about Chronic Fatigue Syndrome, and displayed all of the signs. I never spoke about it to anyone because I was a teenager and thought that people would just think I was being lazy. So, I just sucked it up, and carried on the best way I knew how.

Chapter 4
Suck It Up, Princess

As time went by, I focused on my education and then climbing the corporate ladder, so to speak. Moreover, I was doing great, in spite of the bone crushing fatigue, and strange sensations that would come and go without explanation. My former boss at a building supply company's distribution center used to call me "The Star of the DC". This high praise landed me a promotion to Office Manager at the local retail box store. I worked hard, and I loved it. I got up, went to the gym every morning by 6:00 am, and was ready to open the store for 7:00 am. Rarely did I only work eight hours in a day. It was more common for me to stay until at least 6:00 pm.

Then one Saturday in December of 2001, as I was cleaning out the supply closet at work, I fell off of a ladder, tearing some ligaments in my lower back. I was taken off work, put on Worker's Compensation, and bed rest for a couple of weeks. Those were agonizing weeks. Not just the physical pain that kept me bound to the sofa, but there was a huge struggle in the mind that had to be dealt with. For some reason, all I could think about was getting back to work. It sounds so unimaginable to me now, however in my mind, people at work were incapable of functioning without me. I had little awareness that I was beating myself up for not feeling well, which in turn was making my health worse, as well as hindering any ability for my body to heal. Then it was time to start Canadian Back Rehabilitation. During their initial assessment of me, they found that I had poor balance, measured weakness in my hands, and I dragged my feet as I walked. I attributed the foot dragging to the back injury. The dragging turned into what looked like cross-country skiing, as I could not really lift my legs. Again, I assumed it was from the back injury.

I was in such a rush to heal fast so I could get back to work. I had the business yearly Inventory approaching, which was a basis for my report card, so to speak. I decided that I should try to get back to work for an hour or two per day, in order to prepare for the yearly inventory coming up. I printed off my first report to start the process and discovered that, once again, I could not see out of my left eye. A flood of memories washed over me from 1988, and I realized that this just might be a bigger deal than I thought. I made an appointment with an eye doctor who saw me immediately and explained that my eye problem was "out of her league" so she arranged for me to see another ophthalmologist. He examined me and then booked me for an MRI two days later. I was then sent to a Neurologist. He performed a neurological examination and then sat me down in his office. He attempted to give me a sheet of paper containing four disease-modifying therapies for Multiple Sclerosis. I felt like I was in a dream. I mean, why would he be handing this to me? So I asked him, "Are you telling me that I actually have Multiple Sclerosis?"

"Yes." He replied.

"You're positive?" I asked.

"Yes." he replied again.

He handed me the sheet of paper that contained information about four disease modifying drugs therapies, and told me that I needed to decide which of these four treatments I was going to take and his office would help me get everything all set up.

I do not remember much else about that day, just that I left the neurologist's office and sat in my car, screaming for about an hour. I had to go back to work right after that appointment, so I just screamed until I felt numb enough to go back to work and pretend that everything was okay.

I then went to go see my family doctor and he pulled the report from 1988 by the neurologist at the medical research center. This neurologist was known as the leading authority on Multiple Sclerosis. The diagnosis was "Probable MS. Wait and see."

Chapter 5

Divine Timing

My first thoughts were many, "How could my family doctor not have told me?", "Why didn't my parents tell me?" I felt as though I had been lied to and deceived by the people who were supposed to be taking care of me.

Now my thoughts are, "Thank you, God." Let me explain:

I call it Divine Timing. Of course, the diagnosis was frightening, but let me show you how you can find a silver lining in that dark cloud. Let us pretend for a minute that the doctors had told me that I had probable MS. What would have happened? We will never know, however, I can say that I may or may not have just given up on life. I may or may not have dropped out of school; I may or may not have believed that I was capable of working, which I have done since I started babysitting at age eleven. Would I have gone to college? Would I have found my future husband, or even allowed him to love me? Would I have strived to climb the corporate ladder as I did, earning the promotions? Would I have medical benefits that cover the thousands of dollars in medical expenses? I will never know the answers to those questions, but I can tell you that everything that has happened to me in my life has happened in the precise order of just the right timing, according to God's plan.

Regardless of the circumstances, I have everything that I have needed for my highest care, and that is a blessing!

The diagnosis of Multiple Sclerosis can cause much uncertainty in one's life. All of a sudden, you are labelled with a disability. This means many companies will not hire you. In addition, even if they did, let us not forget the "pre-existing condition", that could put limits on your medical benefits and other insurance policies, if you are even able to get any at all. Here is the amazing part: When I was thirteen, a few months before I experienced that first flare up, my father had purchased a life insurance policy on me from a good friend of his. This gentleman was just starting out in his insurance business and my father was one of his first clients. My dad bought a really good policy on me to help his friend establish his business. Dad even checked off the "waiver of disability" clause, which allows me to purchase insurance from him regardless of pre-existing conditions. Again, this happened a few months before I experienced the first "episode". Funny how his helping a friend ended up being a huge blessing for me. By not knowing about the "probable MS", I was able to complete my education, even achieving a place on the college's Honour Roll. I went on to work for a large and successful corporation, eventually receiving Full Time status complete with Blue Cross benefits. I received promotions that allowed me to grow and stay within the corporation, still with full benefits. I married the love of my life who is the perfect man for me. As it turns out, I have known him most of my life. At each of these moments in life, there was Divine intervention. I have all the time in the world to take care of myself. I have time to help people. I have a pension from the company I worked for to help me pay my way. I have benefits to cover my medical needs, which runs into the tens of thousands per year, paid for, and I have a life insurance policy that cannot be waived due to illness. Moreover, even though I knew my husband for years, it was only when the timing was right that we became a couple.

Know that there is a reason for everything. Imagine how many

Divine interventions we face on a regular basis and are not even aware of it. Let me give you an example, let's say you are driving up the boulevard and running late. It seems that you are getting every red light; a slow poke cuts you off making you even later. Do not get frustrated; instead learn that first, you should have left earlier, and second that you are always in the right place at the right time. Maybe that slow poke who cut you off saved you from being broadsided at an intersection further up the street. Be grateful for every situation that you encounter, and you will be amazed at how much more will show up for you to be grateful for.

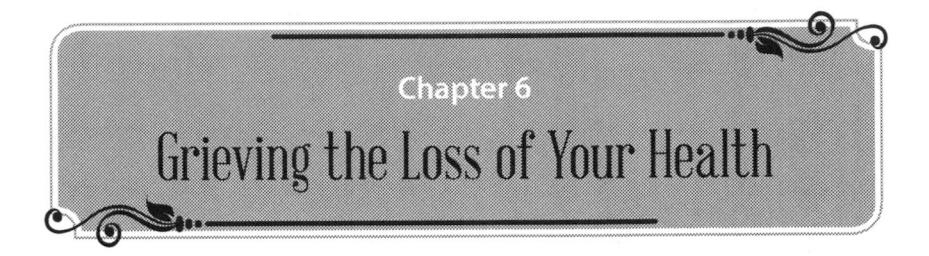

Chapter 6

Grieving the Loss of Your Health

Being diagnosed with Multiple Sclerosis or any chronic illness will teach you many lessons, if you are prepared to listen. For starters, you have been diagnosed with a chronic condition and yes, it does seem unfair. It certainly was not part of your plan, and may leave you asking, "Why me?" Finding out that you are sick invokes many fears for the future, such as employment issues, discrimination, loss of control, and medical expenses. Not to mention the actual demands this illness will take on your body. The vision you once had for your future has been obscured by uncertainty. And all of a sudden, you cannot even bear to think about the future, and what it may hold.

At first, many people go into denial. I know that I did. After the official diagnosis, I can recall one day in particular at work. I had to go retrieve a 10 pound tote from my boss's office. I bent over, lifted the tote, lost my balance, spun around in a funny little dance and landed on my butt. My boss looked at me out of concern and asked if I was okay. I quickly stood up, shook it off, and exclaimed, "I am fine, and I am functioning!" as I sped away.

It suddenly appeared to me that people were treating me as though I was made of fine porcelain. When people find out that you have a chronic illness, everyone wants to help you up the stairs, whether you need the help or not. God bless them all, but people start trying to do things for you. It is hard to appreciate the help that is being offered. To people on the outside, they care for you and are just trying to help. But to you, it feels as though people are noticing your shortcomings and are trying to compensate for what you are no longer able to do on your own. Personally speaking, this led me to the next stage of anger.

Through my eyes, it seemed as though everyone was looking at me differently than before. Some people would look at me and I could actually feel them pitying me. When your peers learn that you have an illness, it is as though they begin to feel sorry for you, and then tell you, "But, you look so good!" You want to answer, "Thanks! I feel like crap!", but instead you bite your tongue, take a breath, and politely smile and say, "Thank you." I found this stage so difficult. I felt as though people did not believe that I was ill, that maybe I was faking. I can remember needing to use my parking pass because my legs burned so badly it was all I could do to put one foot in front of the other. Then I would see people looking at me like, "Where's your wheelchair?!" I mean how can you feel so awful yet look so good at the same time? It just didn't make any sense. Therefore, you keep going and you try to go on as if nothing happened. In my head I thought, "Easy peasy. I've got this under control. Just suck it up." You silently cringe and learn to just say "Thank you," when you are told how wonderful you seem to be doing, no matter how bad you feel. You keep fighting to do all you did before, thinking, "If I could just get this done…" and then find an extreme fatigue setting in every cell of your body. Lesson here is that fatigue will always set in when you are swimming upstream. This is true for everyone, illness or not.

Feeling as though you are fighting a losing battle, you slip into depression. You now see that you can no longer go on the way you always have. You can feel the looks on people's faces when they see you struggling. You thank people for offering their assistance, but silently resent the fact that you are no longer able to do many everyday "normal" things on your own...

The mere act of leaving the house can seem insurmountable, as you know that just getting ready will exhaust you. You end up confining yourself as a shut in. You just want to go to bed and stay there until you can be normal again.

Ending up on Long-Term Disability, as the ripe age of 26, collecting a disability pension which is a fraction of what you earned before, and the possibilities of climbing the cooperate ladder, which had been how I defined personal success, disappeared. Poof... just like that. Gone. I felt hopeless.

Young and on a disability pension just feels so wrong. Still people keep commenting about how good you look. It makes you feel ashamed. I started working at age eleven, babysitting, and I had been steadily employed ever since. I had always been so proud of my work ethic, which I had considered one of my best qualities.

The thing is, many do not understand with Multiple Sclerosis, as well as many other illnesses, is that many of the disabilities are invisible. You cannot see pain. You cannot see fatigue, poor balance, numbness, tingling, or cognitive function to name just a few. I understand and so do many who are living with chronic illness that dealing with all of the above at any given time is not easy. It is taking all of your energy to just physically be there. So I have learned that when someone says, "But, you look so good!" DO NOT FEEL GUILTY! Instead, learn how to change your perspective into feeling blessed that you are handling your difficulties with grace. These people have no idea that just the act of getting out of bed may have taken 20 minutes, not to mention showering, drying your hair, styling it well enough to look presentable, and then layers of makeup attempting to hide the dark bags under your eyes. Add in cooking breakfast, and then driving to your destination and it won't be long until you realize that you have exhausted your energy resources for the entire day before you've even arrived. There is extreme power in changing your perspective. This is what finally brought me to the last stage.

Acceptance, I thought it would never come, and it took several years. I spent the next ten years or so swimming upstream. The doctor had put me off work to avoid stress and to take care of myself. So, what did I do? I tried to find a way to work. The company that I had been working for was really good to me and tried to the best of their ability to accommodate me, however, the simplest of tasks used up every ounce of energy I had. I studied the art of Feng Shui, and tried to be a consultant, with no success. I tried selling Avon. I was really good at it, however the fatigue got to me. I was putting so much effort into selling Avon, instead of following Doctor's orders and taking better care of myself, that it was causing a worsening of symptoms. So next, of course, I tried to start up a website business affiliated with Amazon. com. I learned a lot, however, no success. Once again, I only ending up tiring myself out to the point where my symptoms would begin acting up. Up until recently, I had always based my self-worth on what I DO rather than who I AM.

After being put on long-term disability, I fell into a major depression. Not only did I have Multiple Sclerosis, a few months after the diagnosis my dog died. Then my Nana, who was like a second mother to me and my sister, and had lived with my family since I was 2 years old, died an agonizing death from C. Diff. I was at the hospital every day; I saw her suffer for three agonizing weeks before she finally passed.

I spent the following seven years going from bed to sofa, and sofa back to bed. I had to give myself injections, to which my skin reacted horribly. I looked as though I had tried to make friends with some angry wasps. The medication that I was on left me feeling as though I had a flu, on top of everything else.

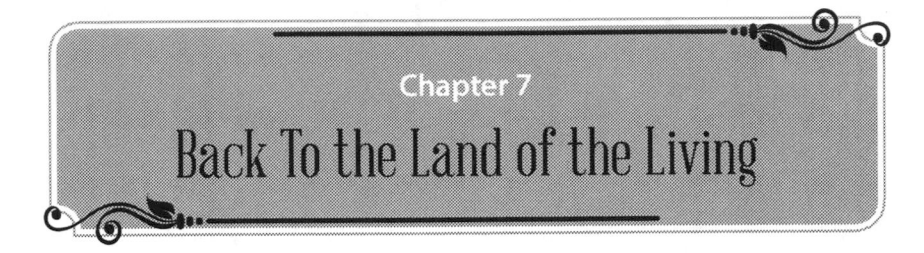

After being on the injections for 7 years, I was introduced to a new drug that was to be administered by a nurse by infusion at a clinic. This was a once a month intravenous treatment, which was my initial reason for switching. The injections had really taken a toll on my skin. I was pleased to find that this drug was better than I expected. I was finally able to get out of bed or off the couch and at least get some housework done, and even a little yoga practice. It was at that time I started to learn Reiki and apply this healing technique to myself. Finally feeling a little better, I began to read all the self-help books I could get my hands on. I spent my time researching all sorts of things and filling my brain with as much as I could process. I learned to meditate, and found the answers in the silence.

Finally, I get it. **Accept what is. Let go of what was. Have faith in what will be.** The truth is that I am a 41 year-old woman who has been living with Multiple Sclerosis for 28 years. That is how I define success today. I am free from the rat race of being a slave to the grind, and I have learned that I can care for myself, in the highest and best ways, and this has sparked my desire to help other people learn from my experiences.

Chapter 8

Be a Good Patient

If you are in the same boat, remember to be a good patient. Always be very kind to people who can legally poke and prod you with sharp objects. Most people in the medical field are generally very busy and rarely stop long enough to actually see you as a real person who is seeking their help. To the average hospital employee, you are just another patient.

For example, let us say that you need to have blood work done. The workers at the hospital see a name, a number, and instructions. They do not see who you are. In their perspectives, they are just at work doing their everyday job. They have their own lives and their own set of circumstances that they are dealing with. You are only a tiny part of their daily routine. There is nothing wrong with that, but let us say you have small veins and it is usually a challenge to draw blood from you. This is a time when you are going to appreciate a little extra care, like a warm Magic Bag on your arms to get your veins ready for injection, if you're really lucky.

When you meet your doctors, nurses, phlebotomists, MRI technicians, etc., SMILE. Introduce yourself and offer to shake hands. Then, find something to compliment on the person who is treating you. Say something that will make them feel good. This may sound hypocritical or as though you are being phony, but remember, these people are working on your body. They will be gentler with you. Also, when you give someone a compliment, it is similar to a blessing. And we all know that when you bless someone, God blesses you. It's a win-win here. You are going to appreciate that little extra care when they have to work on you. Act as though you are trying to be as helpful and cooperative as possible. If you get a needle, thank them for being gentle, whether they were or not. You will be amazed at how your level of care will increase. My grandmother always said, "You get more bees with sugar than you do with vinegar." And she was right.

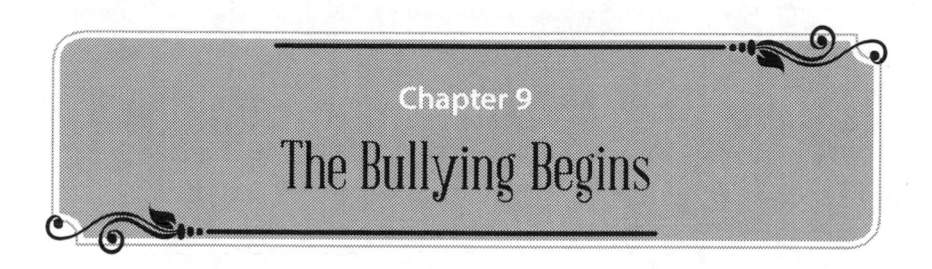

Chapter 9
The Bullying Begins

I stated earlier, I started off alone, fighting to survive. How many times have I been left alone, struggling to find my way? It seemed when I was a child that everyone I had ever looked up to or loved left my life. For example, the Church's music leader, whom I loved as a father figure, moved away when I was about five, and my mother tells me she feels as though I had never gotten over it. My father was a traveling salesman so he was gone for at least half of every week. My childhood best friend, who lived just two houses away from me, moved away at the end of grade 2, after that, the bullying started. I did not have any friends after she left. I gained weight, needed thick glasses, had crooked teeth, was extremely clumsy, and people made fun of me daily. There were only two other overweight girls in my class, as opposed to nowadays. It really sucked to be quite honest. I was called "fatty" and for some reason a "show off". From grades three to six, I had no friends.

One day in grade six, I had called a fellow classmate, we will call her Emily, and asked if I could go play with her. "Sure, come on over." She said as we hung up the phone. A different girl from school called me back immediately from the same phone number. She said to me, "We don't want you to come over and play with us because Emily hates you, and so do I."

Ouch! Feeling the sting, I hung up the phone with tears in my eyes.

My parents were so broken hearted for me that they called that girl's parents, who advised those children to call me back, apologize and invite me over to play. I actually went over. For years, I always thought that was a show of weakness. However, I have a different perspective on that now. I went over there as though nothing had happened, played my heart out, had a great time, in spite of the bitches. I did what I wanted to do, whether they liked it or not. I finally grew some balls!

The following week we were back in school. I recall having to go sharpen my pencil by the teacher's desk, which meant that I had would have to take a walk in front of those same girls. As I walked by, I could hear them saying to each other, "Eww, Michele's germs..." and I watched those girls were pretending to wipe said germs on each other, laughing. That did it, I snapped. I picked up Emily's desk, dumped it out all over the mean girls and threw the desk at them. Emily laid on the ground, looking completely shocked, covered in books, garbage and an empty desk on its side. The teacher exclaimed, "Michele, mudroom, NOW!!!" You could hear the collective "ooooooh" rising from the class. When we reached the mudroom, my teacher told me she was so proud of me for finally standing up for myself. "Now go back in there and act like I gave you shit!" From that day on, she entrusted me to look after her children by babysitting, and provided me with a soft place to fall. This meant so much to me. She became a good friend and was one of the few people who I felt did not judge me, and loved me for who I am. She saw the potential in me when I certainly did not show it to others, especially throughout my teenage years.

Chapter 10

Switch to a Positive Perspective

Most people look at me and think of me as a sweet and innocent person, when nothing could be further from the truth. I am not saying that I am a bad person. I acknowledge that I have made many, many poor decisions and displayed a lot of bad behaviour over the years. Thank God, I have learned a lot from the poor decisions that I made and am finally free to focus on the good things in life. I have been so blessed in this life in spite of myself. God has always had His hand on my life. He turned what was a lonely, sad, depressed, and misunderstood little girl into the woman I am today. I am now in a position that I get to do whatever I feel I need or want to do.

One of the biggest lessons I have learned is that, generally speaking, when people ask you, "Hi! How are you doing?" for the most part, they are expecting to hear, "Great, how are you?" This is called "exchanging pleasantries". No one wants to be around a whiner or chronic complainer. If you start spilling your guts, and complaining, take notice at how quickly people are trying to escape and run in the opposite direction. Stop complaining, put a smile on your face, and be positive. It does not matter how you really feel... saying anything positive will immediately help you feel a little better. Let's call it "Fake It, Until You Make It!" I have finally done this enough that I am no longer "Faking It", and you can do that, too. The more you focus on the negativity in your life and/or body the more you will feel that pain. It is the same when you look for the positivity. When you switch to a positive way of thinking, you begin to change your perspectives, which in fact do create your reality. Just like driving a car, don't look in the ditches or at the perceived obstacles. Look at the road in front of you, or the destination of your desire. You are much more likely to end up where you want to be when you focus on where you want to be. "Energy goes where energy flows."

I can't begin to tell you how many people I have met and known who deal with their problems by constantly spewing about what hurts, how bad, doctor's won't listen to me, blah, blah, ... and I can tell you that I've watched people literally trying to run away from them. Funny thing is, were you to offer advice regarding their problem, they would quickly dismiss you, even if you had the cure, making up some excuse as to why your idea will not help them. Metaphorically speaking, it is as though they have a splinter that hurts them really bad. You have the tools to remove the splinter and help them make their situation a little easier, if not resolved. However, these people will often choose to protect that splinter instead of removing it. They have become so familiar with their pain that if they were to let it go, it is as though they think they will cease to exist. They have incorporated their perceptions into part of their identity. These people also tend to be one-uppers. For example, if you had a cold, they had bronchitis or pneumonia. If you had a headache, they have had recurring migraines. You can try to talk sense to these people, but be warned, they are stubborn. So stubborn that they prefer to hold on to old hurts, grudges, resentments, perceived betrayals, and beliefs. Stop protecting your pain, let it go, and change the lens of the glasses through which you view the world. If you can be stubborn enough to hang on and dwell on that which does not serve your best interest, then you are more than capable of being stubborn enough for your own benefit, and make the changes that are necessary to bring you what you really, really want in your life. You are the only one who can control you and how you choose to live your life.

How do you think you are perceived amongst your peers? Really stop for a minute and think; take a good and honest look at yourself. Are you kind to people? All of the time, or only when you are in a happy state of mind...? Do you look down on certain people or judge others? Have you silently commented to someone about another's appearance or perceived shortcomings? How much fun do you think you are you to be around? Are you fun only some of the time? Do you get moody with certain people? Have you allowed your triggers to trigger you? Identify and be aware of your triggers, because it is possible to change how you feel about them, if you decide to. Be the kind of friend that you want to have. Be the kind of spouse that you want to have. Be the kind of person that you want to be surrounded with.

Another really great lesson that I learned is kindness is usually reciprocated. If you don't believe me, just smile at the next person you see and notice that they cannot help but smile back. The same is also true for unkind people. Are you living with the perspective that people are generally unfriendly? Perhaps you tend to think you see people giving you dirty looks? It could be that they are simply mirroring the look on your face. Not nice to your waiter? Do not be surprised if he spits on your food. If you have a chronic illness, and it is likely that you will be earning frequent flyer miles at your doctor's office or hospital, I urge you to understand the law of projection.

The Law of Projection simply states that what you see in this world is a reflection of what is actually going on in your own mind. Your perceptions on just about everything are based on everything that you have personally learned, observed, and believe to be true. What you see is a product of your subconscious programs and beliefs that are either helping you, or holding you back. I will share with you an experience I had at the local emergency department during the summer of 2012.

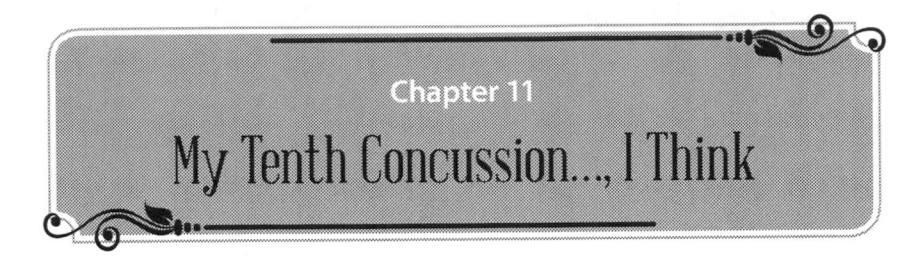

Chapter 11
My Tenth Concussion..., I Think

I had gone over to my friend's house and had a glass of wine. After I came home, I took my dog out for a potty break. He was having a difficult time with stairs at that time so I carried him up the steps. While I was carrying him in the front door, I lost my balance and hit my right eye/forehead on a sharp corner from the shelves at the entrance. I blacked out, eventually got up, puked, and went to bed. When I woke, my eye was purple and swollen shut. My husband was away so I called my father to take me to the hospital, and then he left to go back to the multicultural event that was in town. I was still dressed up from the night before which was an extremely hot and humid evening. The previous week I had received an infusion of the monthly intravenous drug that is prescribed for treating Multiple Sclerosis. I have small, rolling veins, so it took them a few tries to get the IV in place. To the person who did not know me, I probably looked like a junkie with track marks who had been in a bar fight and lost. And that is exactly how I was treated.

People are so quick to judge, going through their lives assuming that everything they think they know must be the absolute truth. The many staff members at the hospital were so wrapped up in their own mundane activities that they did not even bother to read my chart. Even in triage, they think that every person is the same. My normal blood pressure runs around 90/60. When they took my blood pressure, it was 135/90, which is not that significantly elevated for the average person, however, it was for me. I could not see straight. Due to the concussion, I was seeing three of everything, and staggered as though I were drunk. The nurses came and hooked me up to the cardio monitors, and then they wheeled the bed I was in to another room, leaving my clothes and shoes behind in the last room. When I asked for them, I was dismissed, "Don't worry about it." they said. I was told to provide a urine sample, however, the hospital had been newly renovated, and I had no idea where anything was. Nobody showed me where the washroom was, nor did I have a specimen collector in which to place the urine sample. Finally, I got the attention of a ward clerk who kindly gave me a specimen container and helped me to the washroom…still in my bare feet. She advised that if I needed help I could pull the cord. I thanked her, thinking, "Finally, some kindness".

I was wearing a blue paper gown, had heart monitor leads and wires hanging off of my chest and I was seeing three of everything due to the concussion. As you can imagine, getting a urine sample was not an easy task. I had to remove the paper gown so that I could see what I was attempting to do, and I laid it gently over the sink. I then got all the wires attached to my chest monitor out of my way and did the deed. That is when I realized that my paper gown was all wet and ruined because of water droplets in and around the sink. So there I was, wearing only red lace underwear and a heart monitor. I pulled the cord to ask for help. Unfortunately, the kind person is not the one who came to my assistance. It was the nasty one wearing glitter makeup. She leaned between the door threshold and the other hand was on the doorknob, keeping the door wide open for the gentleman across the hall to watch me, in all my naked red lace underwear and heart monitor glory.

"What?" she asked, chewing gum, smirking.

"The paper gown is ruined! I need help!" I cowered against the wall.

She sighed, left the room, door still open, and brought me another paper gown. I graciously thanked her, and as she walked me back to my cell, I tried to hold her arm for balance. She gasped and acted like those girls in grade 6 saying, "Michele's germs!" I remained calm, and got back in bed. Realizing that once again, I was alone and in trouble, I began to cry and pray.

I heard the specimen cart coming and knew she was there to take my blood. Experience has taught me to always be extra kind to people who can legally poke you with sharp instruments. Having had tens of thousands of needles so far, I thought I would be helpful and explain to her that I have small veins that roll. I had not realized that to everyone else, I appeared as a drunken junkie.

"I am not worried about it," she snarled.

She began looking for a vein from which she could draw blood. She looked, and looked, and looked some more.

Finally, I asked her, "Are you worried yet?"

"Nope!" she shouted, as she shoved the needle directly into the vein in my bicep!

"That's going to leave a bruise." She smiled.

I am still amazed at how calm I remained. It hurt badly. I took a big breath in and then I simply explained, "That's okay, it will just match the rest of the bruises," which I now realize she thought were track marks.

"And just where did you get those?" she asked sarcastically.

"At the Coverdale Infusion Clinic." I replied, ever so sweetly.

"What do you go there for?" she starts to look a little funny.

"For IV infusions of medicine to treat Multiple Sclerosis." I replied.

Well, I have heard people talk about when they see the color drain from someone's face, but I had no idea how funny it would look until that moment. In that moment, everything changed. All of a sudden, she was offering me water, food, warm blankets, anything she could think of to make me more comfortable, and probably a little less pissed off. After the diagnosis of a fractured frontal bone, due to loss of balance from Multiple Sclerosis, she was irrationally kind. Even as I was leaving the hospital, she was waving shouting, "Goodbye, Honey! Take care!"

I was not going to tell anyone about her, but I began thinking about how she may treat other people unfairly who may not be as strong or cooperative as I am, or able to stand up for themselves. So I felt compelled to tell the Emergency Department's Manager the next day. She was horrified to hear of my experience and apologized profusely. I insisted she not get in trouble, I knew she had learned a valuable lesson. (At least I hoped.) I hope she never judges anyone ever again, and has learned that she should read patient charts before treating the patient.

In this case, you can tell she had been acting instinctually based on the lessons that she has learned in her life. It truly had nothing to do with me. It was her perception of me that caused her to react to me in the initial way she did, until she heard the truth. And that is an example of the Law of Projection in action.

Chapter 12

Good Days / Bad Days

I tried my best not to complain when I was feeling so awful. However, I don't think I realized just how sick I was until I started to feel better. I got off the regular injections, which I had been on for seven years, and then went on to the monthly infusion. That is when my health started turning around.

I had enrolled in online Reiki classes, and was amazed at how my perspectives began to change. I was beginning to realize that the power to heal was not only possible, but probable. Our bodies are designed to heal. If you were to cut yourself, a series of universally intelligent events would begin to occur. Your cells would instantly react by sending T cells to fight any infection, your blood coagulates to stop the bleeding and cell regenesis starts to happen. I learned the techniques, and really developed my connection to the Creator. I would practice daily on myself and was noticing how much better the Reiki treatments made me feel. I practiced Reiki on a few others and was amazed at how the sessions left the client in such a peaceful state of well-being. I was also shocked by the reactions of people's pets. If they had a cat, their cat would rub on me. It was really funny because apparently this behaviour was not "normal" according to the pet owners. Dogs would gravitate to me. I felt like the "animal whisperer" so I offered free Reiki sessions for pets. I have heard so many wonderful stories and testimonials from people who have requested healing for their animals. One of my fish had developed a brain tumour; it was really gross and sticking out of his head. I wish I had taken a before picture, because the tumour is completely gone. I felt completely honored to have been of service. Even to a fish.

A few years later, I was introduced to another new the drug, which is a potassium channel blocker to help people with Multiple Sclerosis walk better. In order to check the drug's effectiveness, the doctor times you walking a certain number of feet. Then in two weeks, they check your time again. Well, my time was cut in half! For the first time I can remember I felt like I actually owned the feet on the bottom of my legs. So, I entered the Speed Sport Pinup Contest at the 2014 car show at the coliseum. I really wanted to prove to myself that I was getting better. I knew it would be the biggest challenge physically that I had faced in several years. I bought my first pair of high heels in my entire life. That felt awesome! I mean, what girl doesn't love shoes? I was never able to shop for shoes that I liked, I had to focus on being able to walk, and never mind the fashion. My new shoes were black with a leopard print stripe, were a 3 inch heel, but to me it may as well have been 6 inches. I bought a retro-leopard print dress, and felt awesome wearing it. So, I rested up, and practiced walking in my heels. And practiced some more. I just prayed I would not fall on my face in front of the hundreds of people at the Speed Sport Car Show. It was difficult, but I did it! I got my hair and makeup professionally done, and strutted my stuff across that stage in a leopard print dress feeling awesome, and looking fabulous! Even though my legs felt like overcooked spaghetti noodles, I did not collapse until I got to the bottom of the stairs into a chair behind the stage. Mission accomplished! And as exhausting as it was for me, it will be one of my fondest memories. After the contest, people were asking me to pose for pictures with their cars! I felt like a star! I accomplished my goal, and it was an amazing feeling.

If you have a chronic illness, accept that you will experience good days, and some not so good days. My advice is rest up and take care of yourself on your not so good days. This will allow you to be the best version of yourself on your good days. Do not feel guilty for pampering yourself! You are worth it! Treat yourself the way you would treat your sick loved one. When you learn to love yourself, this gets so much easier. I found that the most difficult part of taking care of myself was believing that I deserved it, until I learned to love myself.

When you have a good day, shine, and do not feel guilty. When people tell you, "You look so good!" you can thank them and explain that you take excellent care of yourself. You do not need to share the information that you had to rest up for a couple of days before and after you have made an appearance. If people don't get that, it only shows their ignorance to your situation. You are showing the very best you have to offer by putting your best face forward. Do this for yourself, and never allow anyone to make you feel less than who you really are.

I am not saying you have to do this every day, not at all. Only that if you get up and go out looking and feeling good, own it. You deserve to feel good about yourself.

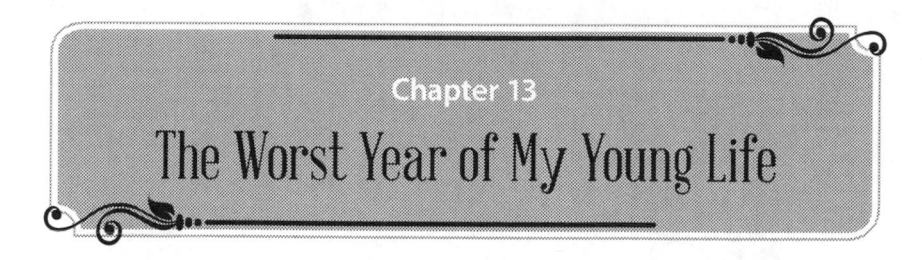

Chapter 13

The Worst Year of My Young Life

I have often wondered about having the onset of Multiple Sclerosis at such an early age. I have heard that it is rare for someone so young to experience this. So, I began looking for possible triggers. I did contract Chicken Pox during the fall of 1987, and then I remembered that 1988 was probably the most stressful time I had experienced to date, and I believe that it was "the straw that broke the camel's back" in regards to developing Multiple Sclerosis.

Have you ever had a memory "re-surface"? I remembered something that I had been lying to myself about since the day it actually happened to me. It was a moment that changed everything I believed about who I thought I was. I was never the same as I was before January of 1988. That was when my teenage world started to crumble. Several close friends of mine became the kind of bullies that shape your persona to the core and write on the slate of who you believe you are. One in particular seemed as though she possessed the power of mob control. Let's call her Sally.

The first time I saw the movie "Dirty Dancing" was at Sally's house. We were very good friends, or so I thought. Mid-term exams were going on at my Middle School, so we only had to be there for our exams, usually a half-day. Sally and I had been hanging out with these older guys from another high school. We all had some good times until I succumbed to peer pressure. Sally dared me to sleep with this older guy we had been hanging around with; actually lose my virginity to a nineteen year old young man after one of my exams. I had recently turned 13. Wanting to be accepted, I agreed and accepted her dare.

I can remember it so clearly now. I was wearing my black faded "bubble gum" jeans, and a pink Cotton Ginny sweatshirt. I was wearing blue glasses and had blonde shoulder length curly hair. He was very sweet and gentlemanly. It was actually a really nice experience. Afraid my parents would see me with him, I asked him to drop me off on the street behind my parent's house. He gave me a hug and a gentle lingering kiss. "You are an amazing girl," he winked. I never saw him again.

The very next day I can only describe as hellish. Instead of me talking to my so-called "BFF's" about what was supposed to be a really big deal for a girl, I walked into a sea of familiar faces, all staring at me. Some were laughing, some were snickering, but all were talking about me. Sally had told everyone, of course, embellishing details that she knew nothing about. I felt like I had shattered into a million pieces. That began a saga of physical, emotional, and mental anguish that became immeasurably hard to deal with. All of my so-called friends had abandoned me; I was seen as a "dirty little slut" and anyone who was seen with me was shamed for it. Unless, of course, it was some guy who wanted to tell people that he had gotten himself a piece of me, to inflate their egos. I can remember one time a guy caught me alone in the stairway of the school. He started "wrestling" with me as though he was playing, until it became obvious he had an agenda. As I was fighting him, he was grabbing at me attempting to violate me, until I managed to fight him off. Then he went off bragging to his friends about the opposite of what really happened. Of course, people are so willing to believe the bad stuff, the juicy piece of gossip that takes their eyes off of their own pathetic circumstances and makes them feel better for a while because the attention is on someone else.

I can remember lunchtimes at the bowling alley. It was the usual lunchtime hangout for most students. I clearly remember all us students walking back to school for afternoon classes, and me walking straight into an ambush. Sally was eagerly waiting to yell at me some more, call me names, anything to try to get me to throw the first punch. We fought. Several times. Teachers would always break it up, eventually. In addition, when it was over, I would see all of those so-called friends just standing there, disappointed that their fun was over. To my surprise, most of the people whom I had once considered to be my best friends were talking crap and accusing me of doing or saying the craziest stuff. Vicious rumours. I am so grateful that social media did not exist back then.

Things had gotten bad enough that I weighed a mere 103 lbs. Every morning my mother would drop me off at school when the bell rang, so I should not have to see anyone before school started. I was late for homeroom every day because my nerves had me stop and throw up in the bathroom on my way to class. Lunchtime, my mom would be there to pick me up and then bring me back to school just in time. Sure enough, lunch rarely stayed down. I remember one time she had to pull over before we got to school because my lunch of chicken noodle soup decided it would rather be on the ground behind the dumpster of a business across the road from school, rather than swirling around in my guts.

So I was labelled as a "bad girl" because I was always getting detention for being late for class. I didn't want to be late, however, the reason I was always late for class was because my nerves wouldn't let me hold any food down. It was a never ending circle. Every morning and afternoon on my way to class, I would get sick, end up late for class, and then get detention. All for trying to protect myself.

Then, all of a sudden, there was this new guy at school. Let's call him "Jeff", and he liked me. Jeff was what one calls an "Alpha" male. He had broad shoulders and seemed more man than boy, as he was sixteen, 2 years older than I was. I thought the sun rose and set on his ass. I would have done anything for him. What I did not realize is that he was friends with Sally. When she found out that he and I were seeing each other, of course the rumour mill churned at full speed. So, in order to protect his "reputation" he told everyone that we were not a couple. However, when not at school, he was all over me like white on rice. He would apologize for being such an asshole to me at school, but if I kept telling people that we were back together, he was going to publicly break up with me.

Still, I thought that I loved him. Worse, I actually thought that he loved me, and that his behaviour was okay. So, I became his "dirty little secret".

One time we were hanging out at one of his friend's house, let's call him "Scott". There was porn on the TV. "Jeff" was always saying something stupid about sexually explicit acts, and then he would attempt to demonstrate on me. Yes, he would force me to have sex with him while people were in the same room, watching porn. It is so sad to see what people will allow to happen in order to feel loved, not knowing that the behaviour is anything but love.

Jeff liked to drink whisky. For some reason, his friend we'll call "Allan" always seemed to have an endless supply of the stuff. One time, we were partying in Allan's basement, and Jeff was drunk on whisky and wanted to have sex. Right there, in the other room. I was so delusional about what being loved actually felt like, and I really did not want to upset Jeff. So, I shot back a few swigs of whisky and off we went.

Jeff and I continued our own little "party" and polished off the rest of the whiskey.

"You know, I didn't pay for this yet," Jeff said as he held up the empty whiskey bottle.

"So what?" I asked.

"Because I need you to pay for me," he replied.

"With what money?" I laughed out loud.

"I'm not asking for your money." he said, as he caressed my face.

I could not believe this. I had to be dreaming. He wanted me to have sex with Allan in exchange for his whiskey! I cried and begged him not to make me do it. He said that it was Allan's first time and I should not ruin it for him by making a fuss.

For years, I had told myself that Allan's mom came home, interrupted everything, and I ran home. I almost believed it was true. Amazing how the mind can play tricks to protect you.

The truth is that Allan's mother did not come home. Jeff was there, Allan was on top of me, and Scott was watching. It happened, and I was powerless. Nobody was going to help me. I was just some dirty little secret, used and abused, left for trash.

When it was over, I rushed all the way home, stopping for nothing. When I got home, I grabbed the bleach, added a cup to the bathwater and soaked until the water was cold. My fingertips had gone white and wrinkly. I even showered off after the bath…I couldn't stand the thought of all that filth on me. I felt so dirty, nothing could make me feel any less corrupted.

Shortly thereafter, in the spring of 1988, I experienced the very first signs of having Multiple Sclerosis. Coincidence?

Chapter 14

The Downward Spiral

Every day it seemed that I had to deal with Sally and her pack of bullies, Jeff and his abuse, having to fight off boys who believed the rumours about me and who would corner me, trying to grope me, an undiagnosed illness that made no sense, and all my parents could focus on was their religion and what the Church leaders were telling them to do in order to cope with me. Nobody ever actually asked me how I felt. The focus was only on how they could stop the stress that they perceived I was putting them through.

I allowed myself to spiral, downward. I didn't feel important. I felt ashamed, and unworthy. Looking for some way to get what I felt was "my power" back; I inadvertently got introduced Black Magic and Satanism from a woman who became the assistant pastor at my parent's church. As she was trying to help people with her story of how she left the satanic world behind, all I could hear was that there was power in it. After all, I was so tired of giving all of my power to Sally and company. Aside from the Sally and Jeff crap, I now had to deal with my sister's shame of me. In my mind's perception at the time, she was the pretty one, she was "the good little Christian girl" that my parents always wished I was. I felt even worse when she would look at me and say, "There it is! I can see the Devil in your eyes!". Of course, my parents believed her... she was the "good" girl. But all I could think was, "What the hell? I am talking, why won't anyone listen to me or even allow me to speak?" How are you supposed to respond to that without wanting to either tell her off or punch her in the face, which would have only served to prove her point? She would also run and cry to Mom and Dad about the latest "nasty rumour" she had heard about me. And yes, there were plenty of rumours, which it seemed that she was using to put the spotlight on how "good" she was versus how "bad" I was. No one ever cared what was actually going on inside of me. Everything became about demons and the demonic surrounding us, preaching fear, fear, and more fear.... I was sick of being sick every day, sick of being used and abused by Sally and Jeff, sick of my parents trying to control the horror that I felt I had to deal with on a daily basis. I felt so alone, bullied at school, no friends, no family that I felt I could talk to because they had all been told that I was a witch, and likely possessed.

Chapter 15
The First Exorcism

The first "exorcism" took place after church, in Riverview. I remember the pastor, kneeling down in front of me, smiling, commanding that I tell him my name "in the name of Jesus!" Really? I couldn't help but laugh. Of course, that was misinterpreted as the Devil laughing in his face. Then the entire congregation all turned, faced me, outstretched their hands, and started speaking in tongues and casting out the "foul spirit". I was only fourteen years old. I snapped. I lost it and told him and everyone there, in the most evil voice I could muster, "Michele's going to hell and we are taking you all with her!" Indeed, I had a flare for the dramatic. (Did I mention that I was voted "Best Actress" in my grade 12 yearbook?) When it was over, again I realized that I had absolutely no one. No friends, no sister, no parents to confide in. Once again feeling alone and helpless, that is when I decided that if it is the Devil they want to see, then it is the Devil I will show. To hear that there was I way that I could get some form of control back and even punish those who hurt me, well sign me up.

I immediately began searching for answers from the darkness. It is such a shame that the darkness is so easily found. Over time, I learned about casting spells, fortune telling, I could even make an Ouija Board out of simple cardboard, and yes, it would work. I became the teenager that you would not want your children to hang around. I showed everyone that I was not to be messed with. I became a bully... the very thing I despised most in the world.

I preyed on the weak, shouting the very same obscenities at people that were shouted at me. I made people cry. I hurt so many people with my bad attitude and poor judgments. I was in a "Do unto others as has been done to you." frame of mind. Still, I was miserable. Secretly, I would remember a person who was hurt and crying after I had been such a mean bully towards them. Deep down I knew that I was only lashing out to try to escape the pain I was feeling. I would remember their faces, distorted with pain and tears running down their cheeks. Instead of feeling vindicated, I felt immeasurable shame that I had been the cause of that pain. I knew that type of pain very well, and I became so ashamed that I had done that to another human being.

I am pleased to report that I did have the opportunity to apologize to those girls for my behaviour. I do not know if my apology was accepted or not, but it was sincere and heartfelt. I know nothing can change what happened; I just pray that those girls were able to heal. I would also like to note that my sister and I have had some very meaningful conversations since then. She said that if she had been my mother she would never have allowed any of that to happen to me. At that moment, I realized my own misperceptions of the past, and how wrong I have been about her. I immediately forgave her and I told her how moved I was at her having said that. She then said that she meant it, and that she loves me. Finally, for the first time I was able to tell her that I love her, too. And I meant it. Now I am so grateful to have her as my sister. I love her and her family very much.

I am going to go out on a limb here and say that I have indeed come to conclude that stress and autoimmune illness go hand in hand. I do not believe that I coincidently experienced the most stressful time of my life just before the onset of Multiple Sclerosis.

Chapter 16
Misguided Religious Beliefs

I was approximately 18 years old when I started becoming aware of my self-destructive behaviour. I eventually renounced evil and also everything that I was taught was evil. I began to understand that if there is power in darkness, then there is infinitely much more power in the Light. Therefore, I turned back to God. NOT RELIGION, let me be perfectly clear about that. There is absolutely no room in my life for organized religion, which I believe was created by man to appease his own ego, and keep you from ever knowing the true Source of all that is. I wanted a relationship with The Creator, like I remembered from when I was very young.

Having renounced the evil, I was welcomed and accepted at church. I had found a wonderful friend at the church, let's call her "Alexandra". Everything seemed to be going okay. Life was getting easier, my relationships with my family were getting better. I had just graduated from high school, class of 1993, and I was ready for the next step.

In March of 1994, a terrible car accident killed my friend, Alexandra. The car she had been riding in to go to work got some slush caught in its tires on the highway, and pulled the car in front of an oncoming transport truck. She was killed instantly. I was devastated. Of all the people I had come to know thus far, she was definitely the kindest and least judgmental person I had ever met.

I remember at her funeral, the pastor was talking about "Why God let this happen to her". He actually claimed that she was taken by God before she could do something to ruin her salvation. "WHAT???!" I could not believe this, yet somehow, the pastor got everyone else to believe it. That began the next chapter I call "The Fear of Eternal Damnation". This fear controlled the next phase of life.

Chapter 17

Demons, Devils, and Spirits, Oh My!

We were taught that demonic beings cling to objects. Everywhere. It could be pictures, ornaments, gemstones, jewelry, and the list goes on. It was all talk about what is evil, and how the devil can so easily deceive you. If I was attracted to a piece of jewelry, I was quickly reminded that the devil loves to look pretty so you'll invite him in. Leaving one to ponder, "Am I being deceived?" all of the time. So much so, that it became an obsession. My mom or church leaders would always remind me, "Watch out because the devil wants to get ya!" They forgot two of the most fundamental lessons: "what I fear - I create", and "darkness cannot exist in the presence of light".

My mother had a large piece of coal that her father had mined in his early years as a coal miner in Minto that had a fossilized plant in it. It weighed about 10 pounds and hung on the wall just outside of my grandmother's bedroom. It was beautiful, and a lovely piece of history from my grandfather. The assistant pastor at my mother's church told her that there was something demonic about it, so mom actually threw it out.

I felt like I was living in a prison. If I didn't give the right amount of money to church, if I wore something with a precious stone on it, if I was wearing a necklace, or if I did not follow the church's teaching to the dotted I's and crossed T's, I was going to pay for it. If not in this life, then the next.

My father left this church, many others also left. My sister and I eventually left, too.

I knew this was not God. This was an egomaniac bent on mind control using the fear of eternal damnation as a tool for his service. This is a very strong fear that limits so many in their abilities to simply trust and believe in The Almighty Source. And you know what I have discovered? If your spirituality is difficult for you, then you aren't doing it right. The most natural relationship that any of us can ever have is with Source of all that is. It is where we came from. I will say it again, religion is a man-made system that is designed to keep you from really knowing God, Source, The Creator of all that is. For example, some Christians think that it is wrong to meditate. I personally believe that praying is you talking to God, and meditating is allowing God and heaven to talk to you.

It was always explained by the church how we needed to have a personal relationship with God, Jesus, or Source, whatever you call it. It baffles me how the church's definition of a "personal relationship" means that everyone's personal relationship should all be identical to theirs. Since when has any personal relationship between two people looked the same as another's? For example, my relationship with my father is different that my sister's relationship with our father. The same goes for our grandparents. No single personal relationship will ever be the same or look like someone else's. We are all individual souls here on our own personal journey.

Religious people who tell you to fear evil have got it wrong. As I said, "What I fear, I create." Our thoughts are that powerful. When you are always watching to see what is wrong, you are self-sabotaging yourself into things being wrong. I realized this one day while noticing symptoms of MS. I have become so aware of every little twitch or physical sensation, that I was looking, almost waiting for the next problem to show. I now see that looking for the problem actually creates the problem. If I thought my vision was blurred, I would end up overstraining my eyes, causing a migraine, and my vision was fine...I was probably staring at a television. But by continually checking and comparing each eye's vision against the view of the other, I ended up causing a separate problem. I have also noticed that this behaviour influences those around you. For example, my dogs were always barking, looking to see what is going to happen next. They were mirroring my behaviour! If I tend to show a neurotic O.C.D. type of behaviour, so will the dogs. So just chill out, relax, and let everything just be as it is, without labels or judgment. The law of attraction works in ways you do not always bargain for. Guard your thoughts!

I affirm that in my world, NOTHING EVER GOES WRONG. I may not like the circumstances that I am in; however, I know it is part of the ever-changing cycle. There is always a lesson or even many lessons for you to learn as you "go through your valley" so to speak. I have also come to realize that sometimes, someone else is being taught a lesson, and although you may be affected by people lashing out in anger, let it go, and realize that most of the time the way people react to you really has nothing to do with you at all. Learn to be content with whatever circumstance you are facing. Learn to be happy now. Only when you are content and release your fears of what will or won't happen will you learn your lesson and then become open to the many gifts from The Universe. When you try to control the outcome of a situation, you are actually getting in the way and may even inadvertently chase away your desired results. Every time that you don't follow your intuition or "gut" feelings and try to take over thinking that you know better, you are basically saying, "God, I don't need your help, I got this." And every time you do that, He will back off, respecting your free will. Do whatever it is that you need to do, inspired action, from moment to moment, and leave the rest up to God and the angels. Think of a flower. It does not struggle to bloom, it just happens as a natural process. When we learn to let go, and just allow life to unfold, without struggling against what is, then miraculous things start to happen. You have the power to make the most out of every situation.

I have seen so many religious people become offended when some say, "Ask the Universe…" Why would anyone be offended by referring to God as The Universe? The Universe is the largest, most awe-inspiring thing that consists of all that ever was and all that ever will be. I ask you this, how is that not the very essence of God? The Great I Am. We are SO limited in our thinking. The Universe is the physical manifestation of God, just as you are. Everything you see around you was all formed by the same space dust that created everything that exists.

Chapter 18
Changing the Channel

I learned to change the recording in my brain. The recording I speak of is that incessant noise that goes on and on in your subconscious; it's the voice that tells you that you are not good enough, or smart enough. That you are fat, unlovable, unworthy, and afraid of everything. The voice in my head used to hold me prisoner until I finally decided by choice to change the background noise in my head. Let me repeat, I decided to consciously change.

I had no idea how I was going to change the noise, but I was determined. And although I certainly did not feel like it, I chose to stop thinking about it and act. I played the song "Happy" by Pharell Williams. I played it over and over again, learning the lyrics, and singing along. It did not happen overnight, but it did not take long. Next thing I knew, I was almost dancing. It was truly amazing. By acting and declaring that "I am happy!" I became happy, and I felt happiness! I ended up singing and dancing to that song every single time I felt less than happy, I used that song as my alarm and also my ring tone. It became my mantra.

Finally in a "happy" frame of mind, I opened myself up to learning as much as I could stuff into my brain. I learned that I really am worthy of all good things; love, joy, health, peace, money, success, etc., they are mine! When you start feeling worthy, you treat yourself with the respect you deserve, which in turns promotes even more health, healing, and self-worth.

I did it! I broke the old pattern, and I created a new one, and I am still creating new patterns as I grow and learn to give up old patterns, thoughts, and behaviours that no longer serve my best interest. I am learning how to not react, but instead when faced with challenges, I am learning to stop, breathe, and observe. Do not react, simply observe. Dig deep, and resist the urge to react. The payoff is that you will finally get out of your own way. You cannot hear divine guidance when you are in a panic or over thinking. By observing, you are able to keep your emotions out of the equation, and will be calm enough to "hear" your intuition. Listen to it... The Creator, and/or angels are talking to us. Just be still, and listen to that inner voice.

Chapter 19

Time Is Only an Illusion

I find it really amusing that there is so much discrepancy over how old the Earth and its many civilizations are. Hypothetically speaking, let us say that "church folk" are indeed correct and that God literally created the entire Earth in 7 days. If that were indeed the case, we could then agree that the Earth is minimally over four thousand years old, right? If we do the math, that would be 4000 years times 52 weeks/per year, which equals two hundred and eight thousand (208,000) weeks since the time of creation. If God rested on the 7th day, then that would lead one to believe that he went back to work on the 8th day, or the 1st day of the following week.

Think about it, if God created the Earth in 7 days (or 7 complete rotations of the Earth), then what do you believe that He has done over the last 1,456,000 days? The ONLY place in the entire universe where a day is measured in 24 hours is here on Earth. We calculate a day by a single revolution of 360 degrees of our planet around its own axis. We calculate a week by counting seven 360-degree revolution cycles. We calculate years based on a 360-degree revolution around the Sun, which takes approximately 365 days, or 365 full rotations of our planet.

To realize this is realizing that linear time, as humans know it, only exists here on this human plane. How can it be any other way?

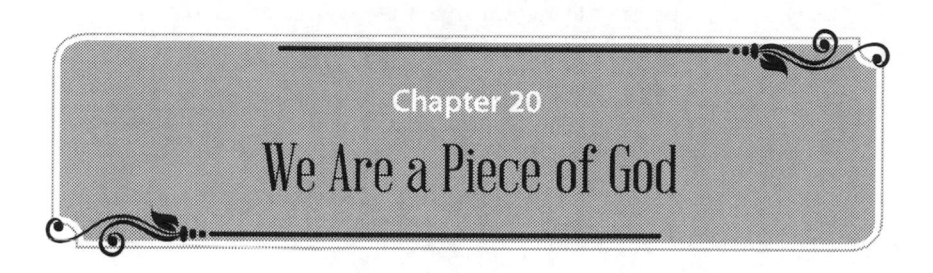

Chapter 20

We Are a Piece of God

We are all created by God. His breath of life, or Spirit, is what animates and gives everyone of us our Divine Spark within…who we really are at the center of our being. When you remove all of life's circumstances, beliefs, and every event that has ever occurred to you…that is who you are. You are NOT your problems, you are not your disease, you are not what you do, and you are not your circumstances. You are a piece of God. He created you as perfect, and regardless of your background, where you are from, what religion you choose, or have been born into, you are His perfect Divine creation.

We could talk forever about how it all began. There is the story of Adam and Eve and "The Fall of Man". According to scripture, Adam's sons were told to go out into new lands to find wives for themselves. Where did these people come from? There are also many books and transcripts, such as "The Book of Enoch", that speaks of angels roaming the Earth, and giants, and the High Priest Melchizedek, and so much more knowledge. Enoch was a son of Adam, who ascended and is now the Archangel Metatron. According to scriptures, Methuselah was the oldest living man at age 969. This puts unknown amounts of time, more than just a thousand years before Biblical history. My point here is that none of us were there. There are archeological finds every day that are evidence that there were giants, lost cities, and so many more wonders just waiting to be found.

I have a perception of the Utopia that was once Earth. In "The Garden Of Eden", we, our souls, were perfect and innocent. Adam and Eve were told to not eat from the Tree of Knowledge of Good and Evil because as innocents, they had no knowledge of good or evil. Think about that. That would mean that they were incapable of seeing or labelling something as "good" or "bad", as the knowledge of good and evil had not yet entered their being. The knowledge of good and evil is what lead humanity into the ego frame of mind. I believe ego is what we should mean when we say sin. Until then, humanity would have been incapable of judging or acting out any of the destructive ego based emotions that had not existed for mankind until they ate the fruit. The result was that their eyes were immediately opened, and their innocence lost. Birth of the ego separated them from God because the ego does not trust, it thinks it knows best. The fruit from that tree contained exactly what is said, "The Knowledge of Good and Evil". Until they gained that knowledge there was no good or evil…everything simply was as it was. Perfect. This is just one of my own personal contemplations on the story of Adam and Eve. It is merely one of the many possibilities.

Understand that you are a Divine creation. Never apologize for who you are. Forgive yourself for all of your perceived transgressions. Know that everything you have been through from the moment of your birth has had something to teach you. See that your mistakes and errors in judgment were all lessons that you needed to learn. Release yourself from self-recrimination. Guilt and shame are feelings that rob you of health and happiness, and you need to release those feelings. Understand that you did what you knew how to do at the time. Hopefully, now you know better, so forgive yourself and know that everything has happened for a reason. There are no coincidences.

When you start to think, "I should have done this", or "I wish I had done that instead.", or "I should not have…" what you are basically saying is that God's plan does not work and your plans are better than God's plan for you. The past is the past, and you cannot change it. You had something to learn from that situation. What is done is done. Forgive yourself and move on. If you are having trouble forgiving, ask yourself why. It is likely that you have not found the lesson you were supposed to learn, and will end up recreating a similar situation that will eventually cause you to learn your lesson. If you believe that hanging on to your past hurts, grudges, and resentments serves you in any way, you are wrong. It is similar to drinking poison and waiting for whomever the resentment or grudge is against to suffer. They don't suffer, you do. In addition, you attract more things to hold a grudge against. And the bitterness and anger can make you sick. Notice how your blood pressure soars when you get angry? How is that hurting anyone but yourself?

Learn to be content with yourself, and grateful for what you have. When you are grateful for something, you attract more to be grateful for. If you've always thought of yourself as, for example, "The poor kid from the wrong side of the tracks with the deaf parents." and you seem incapable of moving past that thought, always feeling as though you don't measure up, you need to understand that that is NOT who you are! That was a circumstance that you have not learned from yet. Let go of all your perceptions, know that everything from your birth on has happened for a reason. You need to start loving yourself, the real you, who you really are, and look for the lessons and blessings that you may have missed at the time.

Take time to examine yourself, and be completely honest. The only thing in this life that any of us have any control over is our thoughts, feelings, and behaviours. Take an inventory of your own thoughts. Are they kind? Do they make you happy? What about your feelings… are you a happy person in general? Why or why not? How do you react to your thoughts and feelings? That is what you control and where your power is. Take the high road and be the mirror reflection of what you would wish for your own self out of every situation. Do not worry about the speck of dust in another's eye while ignoring the log in your own eye.

Chapter 21

Religious Upbringing and Absurdities

Growing up in my family, the topic of religion was one of the most common topics of conversation. My mother had come from a Pentecostal background, and my father came from a United Pentecostal background, which is even stricter. Women were not allowed to wear pants, makeup, or jewelry, other than a wedding ring. Men were to be clean-shaven and have short hair. My father's older sister married a United Pentecostal minister, and they pastor a church to this very day.

Some of my earliest memories at my grand-parents' farm (other than finding out I was allergic to hay) are how the adults would spend many of their evenings. Instead of enjoying each other's company, laughing, and playing board games, the adults would all get their Bibles out and begin what would end up being a several hour long debate over one or two misinterpreted verses from the Bible that defined their religious beliefs. Everybody needed to prove that they were right and that the other was wrong. So, each person would twist and manipulate the Bible verses to match up with their own belief system.

Funny, all of us cousins would sit around in the other room listening to them debate the most ridiculous and unimportant perceptions. Every single one was fighting to be right. At the time, we made fun of them. I can see clearly now how some of us developed our personalities.

I can remember a time when my family had gotten tickets to see a Christian comedian. I will never forget it. He started off his act by shining a bright light on reality. The comedian asked the audience, "How many Catholics are here tonight?"

All the Catholics raised their voices in cheer.

"How many Pentecostals are here tonight?"

Again, the Pentecostals raised their voices in cheer.

"How many Baptists are in the audience?"

Another rise of cheers from the crowd was heard.

"Are there any Mormons in the house tonight?"

More cheers arose from the crowd.

Then the comedian got quiet, and started chuckling to himself. While giggling, he states, "Just think ...SOMEBODY'S wrong!"

Silence.

Very slowly, laughter began to erupt from the huge crowd. It was such an "Aha!" moment for some.

When I was a very young girl, I somehow knew that I was a soul in a human body. Maybe it was those first few days in an incubator, but I can clearly remember a time when I would question, "My brain makes my organs work. So if my brain knows how to work my liver, kidneys, and other organs, why won't it share that information with me, consciously?" I remember feeling very loved by God, Jesus, Angels, etc. I remember at a very young age going up and sitting on God's lap when I was dreaming. I know it sounds crazy, but it was very real to me. It wasn't until I got older that I lost my sight to ego, which inevitably happens to most of us. It is difficult when you are a child, knowing you come from Divine Source, and you see people acting as though what you know to be true inside of you is a lie.

There is a difference between believing something, and knowing something. Believing in something is a conscious choice that you decide for yourself. Beliefs are limiting. If you only believe in what you have been told, it leads to doubting every other possibility that exists.

Knowing comes from deep inside. It is an unshakable truth that nobody had to explain to you. For example, I believed the Bible stories that I had heard in Sunday school. I believed that Jesus loved me. I believed these things because somebody told me. However, knowing is so much deeper. It is unquestionable, you just know. And as a young child, I knew that the highest, most amazing Source that is, loved me, and still does.

I did not see God as an old man with a long white beard and hair, nor did I see Jesus as the pictures described him. As I child, I thought it absolutely ridiculous to portray God that way. I mean, an old man with long white hair and beard did not resemble in any way the Almighty Divine Creator of all that is or ever will be.

I kept what I knew to myself… who was I to argue with my parents or grandparents? So, life went on in the way it always had, with religious people arguing about who was right and who was wrong. This is what led me to really start questioning organized religion at a very early age.

Then one day at the age of eight or nine, the pastor at my parents' church preached a sermon that was so damaging. The title of his sermon was, "God Hates You". Yes, really. I can still see in my mind's eye. The pastor leaning out over his pulpit saying, "Many of you will not like what I am about to say. Most of you will be angry and upset. But God has shown me that you need to hear this message: God… Hates… You!" he said as he slowly pointed his finger at everyone in the congregation. I felt as though every cell in my body was vibrating on a different frequency. He claimed, "God has you hanging by a string over the pit of Hell, and He will laugh as He cuts the string and watches you spiral down into eternal damnation."

That day, it was as though I had shattered and everything was backwards. I was devastated and cried for days. Somehow, though, I knew it couldn't possibly be true. At least I had hoped. I was getting older now and the ego was beginning to take form in me, as sadly, it does with us all.

Over the next several years, I personally witnessed these so-called Christians spread vicious rumours about each other. They made fun of people for being poor. They gossiped about each other, and broke one another's hearts all in the name of religion. Everyone thought that they were right, and others were wrong. In addition, depending on whose side you chose, you could count on the other side coming for you next. I recall later on when I was 11 or 12 years old, one of the church board meetings actually came to physical blows. I have said it before and I will continue to say, nobody can fight like "church folk".

Insanely enough, this madness is still going on to this day. Allow me to tell you about a post that I posted on my Facebook page. The post was a picture of a sign outside of a church somewhere in the Southern United States. The sign simply read, "God prefers kind atheists over hateful Christians". That post was viewed over 34,000 times in just a few days. I could not believe the rhetoric from that post. Most people seemed to get it, the post was simply stating that God would prefer us to be kind to each other instead of mean and hateful, whether you believe in Him or not. I was surprised how so many people had a negative comment about the post because of their need to be offended, and right. Most people who left negative comments were unable to see that they actually agreed with the post, they were just so quick to judge before taking any time for understanding.

We really have to let go of this need to judge. Nobody is better than or less than anyone else. What makes people labelled as 'good' or 'bad' are their intentions. How wonderful would it be if we stopped putting labels on people, and defining them by their circumstances!

I cannot reiterate enough; people, you are not your problems, you are not your religion, you are not your job, you are not what you do, you are not your illnesses, you are not what your geography says you should be, or any other thing you may have used as a label to define yourself. Each of us is a Divine Soul created by God, The Universe, Source, The Creator of All That Is and Ever Will Be. We are all made of the same space dust infused with Divine Light. (Or as I call Him, God) Again, why be offended when someone refers to God as The Universe? I ask this, how could the largest, most awe inspiring vastness that consists of all that ever was and will be not be a description of God, The Almighty?

To me, He has always been formless. Somehow I knew that all of the 'visuals' that were used for teaching tools in Sunday School, or the portraits of God, Jesus, angels, etc., were only a representation of what is true. Even the word "god" is so misused to the point that the word "god" is a mere status symbol rather than resembling anything close to who is The Great I Am.

God is in everything. He is omnipotent, omnipresent, and is in everything that ever was or is today. He is so much more than the human mind can ever comprehend.

Bad things happen to everyone, whether you see them as good or bad is up to you. There is woe in this world. People who are hurting will hurt other people. They are unconsciously trying to unload the hurt they feel onto someone else. Unfortunately, we cannot control the actions of others, only how we choose to deal with our own emotions, thoughts, and feelings. Whatever has happened to you was not your fault. If you were emotionally, physically, or sexually abused, please know that you did not deserve that. If you were bullied, or picked on, know that is not your fault. You did not do something to cause the unhappiness you felt or are feeling. It is your Divine right to be happy.

Chapter 22

Forgiveness for All

The first step to being truly happy is forgiveness. Forgive everyone, especially the people who you don't want to forgive. When you don't forgive, you are holding onto whatever pain you felt. It is as though you are once again protecting that thorn in your finger because it hurts, when the solution is to remove the thorn, or the source of your pain. Unforgiveness can be detrimental to your health and well-being. Please understand that when you forgive, you are not saying that whatever you have faced is okay with you, far from it. You are simply releasing the hold that anger and resentment have on your life. Think of it like this, "I forgive you for being a jerk. This does not mean that you are not a jerk, only that I refuse to dwell on what a jerk you are!"

Once you have decided to forgive others, you need to forgive yourself as well. Free yourself from recrimination of past behaviours. What is past is past. Now you know better and can see that you had a lesson to learn. Keep the lesson, forgive the people and yourself so that you can be free. Whatever you went through, it wrote on the tablet of your mind, and your thoughts are so important. People who feel they have been wronged usually have a negative view of themselves resulting from the poor self-esteem that emotional trauma tends to bring. You need to change the tape that is playing repeatedly in your mind. The things that you notice in other people's behaviours that bother you are usually the things that bother you about yourself. For example, if you think people are gossiping about you, ask yourself, "Who have I been gossiping about?" Another example, you feel everyone is giving you dirty looks; are you smiling, or do you have a scowl on your face? Much of what we think we see is either an illusion of what we expect to get out of life, or a mirror showing us what we've been unable to see in ourselves. This is called The Law of Perception. We see what we want to see according to our beliefs and perceptions. It is the lens through which we view the world. Pay attention to what triggers you because those are the issues you need to work on for self-improvement. Healing can start when you begin to honestly investigate why you are triggered by certain things, or why you perceive something to be as you see it.

I believe that there are physical effects of unforgiveness on our bodies. Let me give a personal example of how unforgiveness can physically cause harm. I know an amazing man who has been successful all of the time I have known him. He has won many awards for Salesman of the Year, and is known as a knowledgeable, generous and strong man. Everywhere he goes, he either finds or makes a new friend. It seemed that for the most part, people loved and admired him. He is also a God fearing man who for some reason feels he needs to live as though he is stuck in The Old Testament of the Bible. He lived in a constant state of guilt as though he was incapable of understanding how much God loves him, even though he will be the first to tell you. Over the years, many people have taken this man for granted. His generosity has been misused and his trust has been broken.

A while ago, he suffered a massive heart attack. When he was sent to the operating room for angioplasty, the doctors discovered a 5-centimetre blood clot in the right coronary artery. This artery supplies most of the blood to your brain. Next, they discovered a seventy-seven percent blockage at the very start of the left anterior descending artery. This artery provides most of the blood to the rest of your heart and body. The doctors are amazed that he is still alive.

Here is where things get weird, but in a very interesting way. The doctors put him on blood thinners for the clot, and cholesterol medication because of the blockages in his arteries. However, when his blood cholesterol was examined, it was lower than any regular healthy patient's should be, and he had absolutely no need for the cholesterol medication. Because cholesterol was not causing the blockage his heart, I truly believe that it was bitterness, and unforgiveness. By not forgiving people who he thought had wronged him, he nearly killed himself. There are many things I could list off that left this man holding onto unimaginable grudges … including and especially against himself. Thankfully, someone who he would actually listen to told him this, and I swear I have not heard him grumble or complain about people who he felt had wronged him since then. I've got to give him an A for effort.

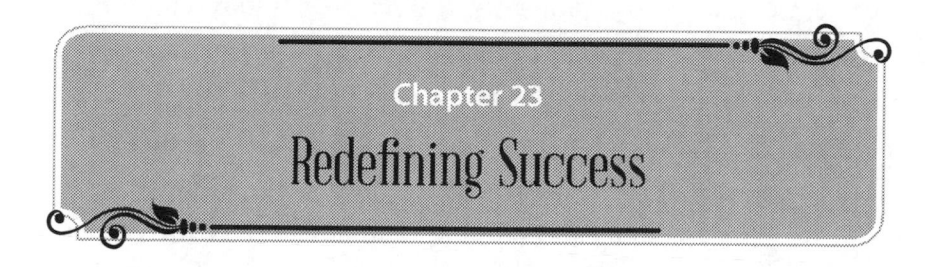

Chapter 23

Redefining Success

I mentioned earlier that I was put on Long Term Disability in the fall of 2002. I spent the next seven years going from bed to couch, and couch to bed. I tried very hard to stay active and was always searching for something, anything to do. I had a very difficult time releasing the need to work really hard for a living, even though I had a new job of taking care of myself. Each time I tried to start a new project to keep me busy, I found myself sick and tired, again.

Finally, it dawned on me. I was listening to a recording by Dr. Wayne Dyer. It said, "If you are what you do, then what are you when you don't do?" I needed to redefine what success was for me. I had been living with Multiple Sclerosis since I was 13 years old. I was a perfectionist, workaholic, and was very busy trying to feel important. Finally, I realized that my job had switched to taking as good of care of myself as I possibly could. Success has been redefined as happy, healthy, and wise. Imagine, the answer was inside me all along. I just had to start being, instead of doing. I came to realize that when I took care of myself, I had a little more energy to get daily chores done. I understand now that my body runs like a car, I have to keep filling up my tank so that I have the fuel to live, love, and laugh. I needed to learn how to love myself, and treat myself the way I would treat a very dear friend.

It was after this revelation that I decided I would learn how to practice yoga. I had a beginner's video series that taught me how to breathe properly. I was completely amazed at how the simple act of conscious breathing can help you hold what seem to be impossible poses. Aside from improved physical strength and flexibility, I realized that I possessed the ability to quiet my mind by simply focusing on my breathing. Finally, I could stop the noise and insanity of thoughts and worries about everything and nothing at all. I could actually work on my ability to focus on what I choose to think about. Our thoughts, feelings, and behaviours are really the only thing that any of us can control.

Chapter 24

Spiritual Awakening

I knew I was onto something. I had heard of "meditating", however I had not given it much thought because the Church always told us this was "New Age" behaviour, and that must be bad. Then I remembered a Bible verse, Philippians 4:8(NIV), "Finally brothers and sisters, whatever is true, whatever is noble, whatever is right, whatever is pure, whatever is lovely, whatever is admirable - if anything is excellent or praiseworthy - think about such things."

In other words, think positively. Think about good things. Think about the things that bring you joy and invoke those warm, fuzzy feelings in you.

Another verse, Isaiah 40:31 (NIV), "But those who hope in the Lord will renew their strength, they will soar on wings like eagles; they will run and not grow weary, they will walk and not be faint."

My interpretation is wait, be still, and open your mind for Spirit to connect with you and give you strength. Be inspired with the sudden clarity that comes in the silence. Allow yourself to be blessed and just connect with the Creator. There is no better feeling than connecting to the Creator of All That Is.

Another, Psalms 46:10 (NIV), "Be still and know that I Am God."

It became apparent to me that we are supposed to meditate, so I began to meditate on my own. I would get comfortable and make sure that there were no distractions. I would close my eyes and become aware of my breathing. Breathe in slowly through the nose to a count of four, hold it for a count of four, and then out through the mouth to a count of four, and another count to four before the next inhalation. All you focus on is your breath. Feel your lungs expand. Just be.

Once this became easy for me, and I no longer needed to count, I found I needed something to focus on or else my mind would wander. So, I learned to bring my attention to my fingertips. I would just focus on trying to feel them, and if any thoughts tried to creep in, I would simply acknowledge the thought, then lovingly and without judgment, let it go and bring the focus back on to my fingertips.

It was like having a mini vacation. I always felt more authentic, calm, centered, and peaceful after meditating. I noticed my overall health improving, as well as my relationships with friends and loved ones. I felt like I came home, if that makes any sense.

Shortly after learning how to meditate, I discovered Reiki, an ancient art of healing, and began learning how to practice Reiki. I studied all three levels earning my Master's Degree in theory. I have mainly practiced on myself, on my husband, a couple of acquaintances, and my pets. I am looking forward to learning more about healing and being of service to anyone who comes to see me for a healing.

There are five principles in Reiki that everybody can use and benefit from:

1. Just for today, I will not be angry.
2. Just for today, I will not worry.
3. Just for today, I will do my work honestly.
4. Just for today, I will be kind to every living creature.
5. Just for today, I will give thanks for my many blessings.

Notice that all five of these principles start with "Just for today," The reason is that most people find that they can commit to something for just a day. Some may need to slow it down to "Just for this minute." If we could learn to adopt these principles and apply them in everyday life, we would find so much more peace. If you need to take things minute by minute, that is okay. If you feel that you got off track, you can easily get back on track by re-affirming which ever principle you believe you need to work on. You cannot make a mistake. Just be gentle with yourself and get back into the flow. It is difficult to commit to not every worry again, but you can commit to not do it for a minute. Then the minutes eventually grow into hours, and hours into a day, and so on.

When you allow yourself to get angry about something or at someone, you give your power away to what has angered you. Anger does not change your situation, but it will raise your blood pressure, weaken your immune system, and lead way to illness. Anger keeps you from seeing the bigger picture, and robs you of your health and vitality.

When you feel yourself starting to worry, ask yourself this, "When has worrying about anything ever solved a single problem for you?" You know the answer. It has never helped a single bit. Of course not. Worry is a complete waste of time and valuable energy. It does not, nor can it solve anything. Worry steals your joy and keeps you very busy doing nothing.

Doing your work honestly is not necessarily about your job or career. This is about being true to yourself, having integrity, respecting others, and living authentically.

Be kind to everyone, humans, animals, insects, and plants, every living thing regardless of how they act toward you or who you have judged them to be. Give up the need to judge anything that you do not like, understand, or agree with. We are all in this together, no one has asked for your judgment. Be kind. The more kindness you give to others, the more kindness you will receive from others.

Give thanks for your many blessings. You may not be focused on what you do have to be grateful for, but look around and you will find many blessings. I found that keeping a list helps me to focus on the good things in life. For example, I have a wonderful husband who loves me. I have a roof over my head, electricity to give me heat, warm water, and light. I have food in my pantry and food in my refrigerator. I have two vehicles that are paid in full in my driveway. I have a pension to help cover my living expenses, and I have Blue Cross benefits that are covering approximately $70,000/year in health expenses. I am free to care for myself in every way I desire. The list could go on and on. I count my blessings regularly and am so grateful for the life that I have been given.

Chapter 25

Words of Wisdom

"Anything that annoys you is teaching you patience. Anyone who abandons you is teaching you how to stand up on your own two feet. Anything that angers you is teaching you forgiveness and compassion. Anything that has power over you is teaching you how to take your power back. Anything you hate is teaching you unconditional love. Anything you fear is teaching you courage to overcome your fear. Anything you can't control is teaching you how to let go." -TheMindUnleashed.

I now know what I wish I had known when I was first diagnosed and put off of work, there is nothing to fear. To the doctors who said I would have a low quality of life and probably be in a wheelchair by now, you were mistaken. To the people who thought it was okay to use and abuse me, I have risen above, and I thank you for the lessons. To the religious people who have come in and out of my life, thank you for teaching me that I am nothing like you, and God loves me anyways. Lastly, I will thank Multiple Sclerosis for teaching me that I can heal, how to be patient, for increased levels of compassion, and showing me how strong I truly am, that the only thing to fear truly is fear, itself. I am grateful that I have learned my lessons, how to honour my body, and I now release Multiple Sclerosis from my body, and my identity.

Romans 8:11 (NIV) "And if the Spirit of Him who raised Jesus from the dead is living in you, He who raised Christ from the dead will also give life to your mortal bodies because of His Spirit who lives in you." This verse speaks to me, as it recognizes that there is a difference between mortality and spirit in all of us. I think it means that God, Source, the Universe's, spirit will inspire and rejuvenate your body and bring healing to your soul. This Spirit is alive and awakening all of humanity now.

I believe these are the days spoken of in Matthew 24:6, 7 (NIV), (6) "You will hear of wars and rumours of wars, but see to it that you are not alarmed. Such things must happen, but the end is still to come. (7) Nation will rise against nation, and kingdom against kingdom. There will be famines and earthquakes in various places." Many have also called these The Last Days.

What did Jesus say would happen in the last days? Acts 2:17 (NIV) says, "In the last days, God says, I will pour out my Spirit on all people. Your sons and daughters will prophesy, your young men will see visions, your old men will dream dreams." Also, let us look at John 14:12 (NIV), which says, "Very truly I tell you, whoever believes in me will do the works I have been doing, and they will do even greater things than these, because I am going to the Father." Not to mention the twenty some other verses that tell us that believers will lay hands on the sick and they will recover.

I believe that this is happening now and religious people are refusing to embrace this because it means that they have to forget everything they thought was truth and be open to change. God does not change, but creation is always changing. I know that these are the times when we will do greater works than Jesus performed. This is not to say that any of us is better than Jesus is, just that the works are greater because of the vast amount of tools that are available today.

Chapter 26

God Has Sent His Angels to Help You

I have personally learned that I can call on Angels to help, heal, strengthen, comfort, and give signs. First, I create a bright ball of light by visualizing it, and by breathing. As I breathe, I watch the ball of light get bigger and bigger until I am in the center of the ball of light, and it radiates 100 feet around me. This light can be bright white, green, pink, or blue.

It is like being in the center of the Sun, but better. I can see the coloured light swirling around me. The energy swirls around much the same way we see pictures on our Sun's cold fusion swirling and floating up and out into the coronal mass. There are angels all around me. In addition, I just allow myself to breathe in the light energy. The energy swirling inside cleanses, removes blockages, and negativity. Then I breathe out from my mouth, and any negativity floats out and away, disappearing into the light, and floating towards the corona. I can see what appears as sunspots of the surface of the ball of light. Sometimes I can even see what appears as a coronal mass ejection as the negative energy goes away.

I know this is my personal visualization, and is mine alone. Other people have their own visions, feelings, and experiences; I just shared mine with you.

I have heard it stated that a bamboo seed needs years to germinate before it will sprout, and begin its growth. However, once the growth process has begun, bamboo can grow more than a foot per day. I realized that I have been germinating for years now, and am beginning to grow. I feed myself healthy doses of Dr. Wayne Dyer, Doreen Virtue and her Angel Therapy, and Eckhart Tolle. I also love listening to the wisdom of Dr. Deepak Chopra and Abraham Hicks. There is an audio meditation from Dr. Wayne Dyer titled "101 Ways to Transform Your Life" which has taught me how to "catch" myself when I act out of ego instead of love.

Looking back on the life I have lived thus far, seeing that I had been germinating all this time, I now see that the momentum has shifted from germination into spiritual growth. I am reading, studying, and writing so I can continue to grow and share my experiences with others. I wish to bring love, compassion, healing, and good advice to help others through their own personal journey through illness and troubles and help people realize their own spiritual path, and know that we are, every one of us, a piece of the Divine Creator.

Chapter 27
Precious Gifts from Both Grandmothers

I mentioned earlier that I grew up in a fundamentally religious family. Both of my grandmothers have passed on, and they both left me a gift of spiritual insight before they died.

My grandmother, who was my father's mother, was a special woman. She loved all of her grandchildren; however, I always thought that she did not particularly like me. Mainly due to my poor judgments and bad behaviour. I have explained some of the teenage torment that I put my parents through, and I could only imagine her perception of me. My father is one who tends to wear his heart on his sleeve and I know that every time I hurt him, he would confide in her. I assumed that she believed the absolute worst about me. And, I did not blame her; I certainly made it quite difficult to be around me.

In 1999, she was diagnosed with a brain tumour, which she fought until the spring of 2000. Two weeks before her passing, my father and I went to visit her and say our final "goodbyes". She had been unconscious for a few weeks at this point and was not expected to wake up; it was just a matter of time.

I went in to see her. She lay there, in a coma, and I spilled my guts. I held her hand and I told her how very sorry I was. I said, "Nana, I am so very sorry I was so mean. I am sorry for all the pain and worry that I have caused. Please forgive me.", I cried.

That miraculous moment is burned forever in my heart and memory. As I cried, she suddenly squeezed my hand; her eyes sprang open looking frantically around. "I love you, Dear, I love you!" In that instant I realized that she understood now what unconditional love and forgiveness truly is, and was sending some to me!

This lasted for about 30 seconds, such an amazing 30 seconds. She never woke again. My aunt who had been caring for Nanny was shocked.

"Wow...she hasn't woken up for over a week!" she exclaimed. "What a special moment for you!"

She had no idea.

I mentioned my mother's mother who suffered for 3 weeks from the super bug C.Diff. We watched her suffer and slowly fade away. On the night of her passing, we knew her death was imminent. After she had been put into a morphine coma, all of the family members gathered around her bedside. We held hands and sang "Amazing Grace". At approximately 11 pm, a nurse came in her room to change her. The family and I were all down the hall, waiting for her to pass. All of a sudden, we could hear her shouting, "I love everybody! I love everybody!"

Immediately, we all sprang down the hall and into her room. Her face had changed; I believe it is what people call "the mask of death". But, her eyes were never more vibrant than they were at that moment. She told us that it is okay. Jesus is waiting for her, and so is Belmore, her husband who had passed twenty years earlier, and her daughter, who had passed exactly 1 year to the date. She looked eager to get back to them, as though some Divine secret had been revealed to her and she finally got it.

She told each and every one of us that she loved us, and slipped back into the coma. She passed peacefully a few hours later.

These experiences bring me to tears every time I think of them. Not tears of sadness, but tears of joy and gratitude. I feel so blessed to have received these precious gifts. It was confirmation for me that the real truth is out there. That unconditional love is all that really matters in the end.

I choose not to wait until my end for this unconditional love to shine through me. I choose to show it now. There is no other time that exists other than now. Now is all we have. I choose love. I hope you will, too.

Chapter 28

New Ways of Thinking

I had never seen either of my grandmothers, nor anyone else for that matter, display such raw emotion in their eyes. The look that was on each of their faces was so revealing to me. I could tell that they were in complete awe and amazement of whatever it was that they had been experiencing while they were unconscious, and preparing for what would come next. Having realized this, I knew that I had to investigate.

I became so intrigued at what I was discovering. I found that, bottom line, science and spirituality actually do agree with each other to a rather large degree. It is only the labels that are different. Having the human need to label and judge is what has kept people from being open to this concept. This world is a world of duality, (up - down, left - right, north - south, black - white). It is the duality of this world that causes man to separate science and spirituality.

For example, dictionary.com states that Astronomy is the scientific study of the universe and the objects in it, including stars, planets, nebulae, and galaxies. Astrology, in contrast, is the study that assumes and attempts to interpret the influence of the heavenly bodies on human affairs. Astronomy is accepted by people because you can look up and see the sun, moon, and stars. It is something that we can physically see, and we have science to support that much more than what our physical eyes are capable of seeing is out there. On the other hand, astrology focuses on how this science affects us. It would be correct then to say that astronomical events affect astrological behaviours. There is no scientific proof to explain astrology, which is why it gets overlooked by many, or thought of as mythical.

I believe we could all agree that the moon controls the tides all over the Earth. This is an example of an astronomical event causing an astrological impact, manifesting in the oceans. We know that a Super moon is a full moon that is much closer to Earth than normal. We also know that this astronomical event, affects the levels of the tides. Adding to this, the human body is over 70% water. We know the moon affects water. Ask any person in emergency medicine, the police, or any other first responder, and they would agree that they are much busier during a full moon.

Many people also talk of the Mercury retrograde phenomenon. This happens when the planet Mercury is in a place where it seems to be traveling away from the Earth as opposed to towards it. It is an illusion, and a cycle that happens every few months or so. Because the Earth travels at a much faster speed around the Sun than Mercury does, we pass by it in orbit. If you were to look at it through a telescope, Mercury would appear to be moving backwards, away from Earth. During this retrograde period, many people will find trouble with travel plans, miscommunications, and technology going awry. Here is the best example I can think of for technology going awry: United States President Barrack Obama launched the website HealthCare. gov on October 1, 2013. Everyone in America was to go online and sign up for The Affordable Care Act, also known as "Obamacare". Do you remember the chaos that happened? To this day people are still complaining about it. The website actually crashed, as I understood it, and nobody had a clue what to do or even how to enroll. Guess what? That was all during a period of Mercury Retrograde. I could list hundreds of examples of travel delays, cars breaking down, computers freezing or crashing, and the Internet being slow and a little "off". I have even had to get the phone line in my home replaced because I was hearing static and echoes. Yes, it was smack dab in the middle of a Mercury Retrograde cycle. My last example, is a person, who will remain nameless, bought a car during a Mercury Retrograde cycle. He had been told that it would be in his best interest to wait a few weeks, however, impatience got the better of him. He never was able to find out what all the clinking and humming noises were, and he ended up with a lemon that needed service more than any vehicle he had ever owned.

Understanding of how the cycle works is the key to getting through the cycle without frustration, and maybe leaving you a little better off. Be prepared that traffic just may be backed up, so give yourself extra time to get to your destination. If you have to make any purchases for example, a home, or vehicles, or electronics, read the fine print and proceed with caution. It is always a great time to review your projects and your life to see what is working for you, and what you may need to change moving forward.

Chapter 29

The Law of Vibration

High School science explains to us that every single thing vibrates. Everything that we can feel, see, smell, touch, taste, is a group of energy vibrating at a certain frequency. For example, the chair you are sitting in is a bunch of molecules vibrating at the frequency of a chair. Matter is essentially a group of vibrating atoms. This vibration of the atoms is the energy that is neither created, nor destroyed; it simply changes form. Do you remember what an atom looks like? All of the atoms in the Periodic Table of Elements look like tiny solar systems. So, we can take a bunch of atoms and form them into a group, creating a substance that has now become a molecule. We can take the molecules and create a cell. Perhaps we could look at a cell the way we would look at a Galaxy. A galaxy contains stars, planets, comets, dust, nebulae, black holes, etc. A cell contains mitochondria, a nucleus, cytoplasm, etc. Just as there are many types of galaxies, there are many types of cells. Cells are similar to tiny galaxies. There are trillions of cells in the human body, and we know that there are billions to an infinite number of galaxies in space. Keeping this comparison in mind, if a human is a body made from trillions of cells, and the universe is a "space" full of galaxies and dark matter, doesn't that make you think of a body? God made man in His image, right? We live in this universal body that I believe is God, showing us that we really, truly, are one. Now we know we are part of this amazing Universe, where everything vibrates.

The Universe is similar to one huge, enormous body. We are but a particle in the vastness of All That Is. In this universal body of vastness, galaxies do not argue with other galaxies. Nor do stars fight amongst themselves. The particles of space do not fight with each other. There is no bullying of other particles or spreading of hate. The planets in our solar system don't hate other planets in our solar system or any other that exists. The Universal consciousness is that of connectedness. Everything works in in perfect harmony. We are all a part of the same space dust that exists throughout the universe. There is no such thing as being separate.

This is something that the human race needs to understand. There is no room for separateness, nor hatred towards another. To hate another is to hate yourself. We are all Divine souls having a human experience on Earth.

Imagine, if you will, what would happen to your whole body if your kidneys hated your liver? Your body would be completely out of alignment and get really sick really fast. Imagine, what if your lungs and heart despised the blood that was being pumped through them? How could you even survive let alone extract nourishment from your blood? We need to function collectively as one body. Without racism, hatred, judgement, and division of classes. I believe that we would experience a kind of utopia with people loving each other all over the world.

Do you realize that we vibrate, too? We are a part of All That Is, so we must. Like vibrations and frequencies attract like vibrations and frequencies. We put out a vibration based upon how we feel. It is similar to us having an antenna broadcasting our frequency to the Universe. I think it safe to say that happy people vibrate at a level that brings more of what they are happy for. The same duality I wrote of works here, if a person is in a bad mood, and feeling anger, guilt, frustration, shame, depression, etc., they will emit a much lower vibrational frequency, attracting even more of the lower energy feelings to them. Figuratively speaking, it is as though we are walking magnets, attracting more of what aligns in our vibrational field. This causes me to be very aware of my personal thoughts, feelings, and behaviours. I know that I want good things, so that is where I choose to focus.

For example, let us say that I have 4 projects on the go, and 3 of them are going very well, but the 4th is failing. So I take my focus away from the successful ones out of fear of losing the 4th. That would put my vibration into a state where I would be broadcasting a frequency of "fear of losing". What do you think would happen? The panic and fear over losing the 4th project would attract more "fear of losing" vibration and then the 3 other projects that had been doing so well may all of a sudden not have the proper care and attention that they had become accustomed to and then they may start to suffer as a result. Sure, my intention was to have 4 successful projects. However, my vibration was not one of success, but of someone who fears losing, so I inadvertently attracted the loss of success for the projects. Instead of panicking and becoming fearful of a loss, I should simply observe the project and focus on what I can do to help, without any fear. Then do what is necessary and within your range of ability, without worrying about the situation, and detach from the outcome. We have all heard the saying that a watched pot never boils. Let it go. Then go back and tend to the first 3 projects, appreciating how successful they are. Your vibration is in your feeling. Feel the feelings that you wish to receive out of your greatest desires, and the world around you will change. By detaching from the outcome, it would be safe to assume that the 4th project had turned out successful because you put your focus into feeling good about the successful projects, attracting more success.

Science has proved how our beliefs affect our reality. Our beliefs that we are conscious of make up only between 5 - 10% of our feelings in our vibrational energy field. The other 90 – 95% is the subconscious mind running in the background. We hold our belief programs in both, our conscious and our subconscious mind. Our subconscious mind does not do the thinking, it is similar to a tape recorder playing over and over again. When we learn to walk, talk, drive, etc., the programme is stored in our subconscious so that we don't have to think about how to walk, we just do it. We don't have to consciously think about every step necessary to start the car, and get from point A to point B, we just get in and drive. A dancer who has trained in ballet all of her life does not have to think about how to dance, the programme is in her subconscious and she just dances. If your conscious life doesn't resemble what you really want, then it is safe to say that your subconscious is holding onto belief programs that are not in your best interest. It is not your fault...our subconscious has a primary job of keeping us safe, without discriminating on how it does so.

Many people use affirmations trying to bring about the change they desire. Using affirmations is great, don't get me wrong, but you repeat affirmations using only 5 – 10% of your mind, and have the 90 – 95% subconscious that may not believe the affirmation you are trying to imbed in your mind. So, if you are a sick person, you can affirm, "I am healthy" until the proverbial cows come home. However, if 90% of you doesn't believe that you deserve it, or if you believe that being sick is serving you, keeping you safe, then all of the positive affirmations you can muster may help to some degree, but it is your beliefs that will shape your perception of reality.

Looking now from this perspective, I can clearly see how my old beliefs shaped my experiences. The experiences that I lived through then solidified those beliefs. When I was first born, I was put into an incubator, with tubes and needles, for 9 days. This taught my subconscious that I got love and attention from being sick. The next time I felt that I needed love or attention, my body would create some sort of discomfort to get the love and attention that I was craving. I was born fighting to survive and my subconscious had decided that illness was a means for survival because in reality, it worked in a twisted sort of way. When I was being bullied, my subconscious remembered that illness was a great tool for survival, so my subconscious conjured more illness in an effort to keep me safe. Having no real idea of what it meant to love myself, my subconscious was completely okay with me sacrificing my body. Of course, it all makes sense now that love hurt. My subconscious was convinced of this. My subconscious then decided that the best way for me to survive was to work harder, and play harder. This brought me success in my career, at the price of my health. I was trying so hard because my subconscious believed that I had to work really hard. I let people use me, and treat me in a way that left me feeling like a failure and unworthy of any good things. Exhausted and tired of fighting, my subconscious created autoimmune issues, thinking it was keeping me safe, and getting people to leave me alone. Then, the cumulative effects ultimately manifested into the autoimmune giant, Multiple Sclerosis.

Now, I have changed those subconscious beliefs. I have unconditional love and compassion for myself. I can clearly see now that every single bully I ever faced was a direct reflection of how I felt about myself and what I believed that I deserved. The really good news is that I know that if I created Multiple Sclerosis, then surely I can dis-create it, and I can create a new reality for myself by addressing my subconscious mind and digging for beliefs that do not align with what I desire in my life.

We are always creating. All of the time. How you feel will influence what you create as your reality. Do you remember the story about "Willie Wonka"? He was a very cheerful and silly man who created the most delicious chocolate and candy. Everybody loved his chocolates. Eventually, a situation arose where Willie Wonka was feeling rather depressed. While in this depressed state of mind, he was unable to make his signature delicious chocolate. None of the chocolate or candy was turning out the way he wanted.

Saddened by his inability to create what he desired, Willie Wonka goes to his therapist, where he has this epiphany, "When I am feeling good and happy, I create the most delicious chocolate. However, when I feel terrible, I create terrible tasting chocolate." Your feelings attract more to you that will make you feel the way you are feeling, so focus on things that make you happy, bring you joy, and cause you to feel wonderful warm, fuzzy feelings.

Take a look at your life. Chances are that if your reality is not matching your desires, something is out of alignment. You get to choose how you will proceed. You can do nothing, and have nothing change, or you can step up and take charge of your life. This life is a gift. Take time to be present and notice the beauty all around you. Allow yourself to feel good and drink in the inspiration that can only come in the present moment. When you start to focus on the feelings that enjoying the present moment bring, your life will begin to change. There is a physical law explaining that an object in motion increases in motion and in momentum, while an object at rest stays at rest. You have the power. It is your birthright. Take it, and soar.

Acknowledgements

I wish to thank my amazing husband for tirelessly caring for my every need. Words could never explain how wonderful you are, and how much I love you. Thank you for loving all of me.

I wish to thank my family, Mom, Dad, Sis, I love you. If it weren't for you, I would not be here today. Thank you for loving me in spite of myself, and for putting up with my shenanigans over the years.

I would also like to thank my friends, you all know who you are. Your support and friendships have helped me become who I am today, and I am eternally grateful for each one of you.

THANK YOU

Printed in the United States
By Bookmasters